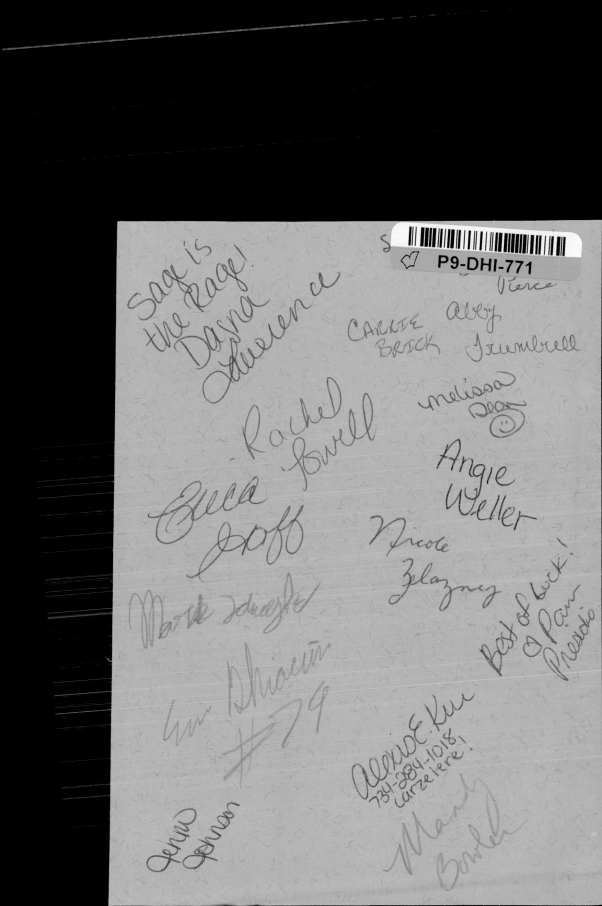

Sage is the Rage!

Dasha

Lawrence

S

Pierce

CARRIE BRICK

Avery Trumbull

Rachel Powell

melissa Dean

Erica Goff

Angie Weller

Nicole Zelazney

Mark Schaefer

Best of luck! Pam Presidio

Gm Dhiacin

#79

ALEXIDE Ker 734-284-1018 carzeiere!

Jenn Johnson

Mandy Bonda

Congratulations
on Oak!
thanks for being a
Part of the Rage!
Have a great time at CMU!

Tiffany Fuller

Congratulations
Look forward to seeing
you in the fall.
Brandon
Green

Lisa—
Good luck,
study hard, +
enjoy every moment.
Damon
Sloan

LIFE LESSONS
MY MOTHER
TAUGHT ME

Jeremy P. Tarcher / Putnam • a member of Penguin Putnam Inc. • New York

LIFE LESSONS
MY MOTHER
TAUGHT ME

Andrea Young

Most Tarcher/Putnam books are available at special quantity discounts for bulk purchases for sales promotions, premiums, fund-raising, and educational needs. Special books or book excerpts also can be created to fit specific needs. For details, write Putnam Special Markets, 375 Hudson Street, New York, NY 10014.

JEREMY P. TARCHER/PUTNAM
a member of
Penguin Putnam Inc.
375 Hudson Street
New York, NY 10014
www.penguinputnam.com

Library of Congress Cataloging-in-Publication Data

Young, Andrea, date.
Life lessons my mother taught me / by Andrea Young.
p.   cm.
ISBN 1-58542-007-7
1. Young, Jean Childs—Philosophy.   2. Young, Jean Childs—Anecdotes.
3. Afro-American women—Conduct of life.   4. Afro-American mothers—
Biography—Anecdotes.   5. Young, Andrea, date.   6. Daughters—United States—
Biography—Anecdotes.   7. Young, Andrew, date. —Family.   I. Title.
E840.8.Y647 Y68   2000   99-051694 CIP
973.92'092—dc21
[B]

Printed in the United States of America
1   3   5   7   9   10   8   6   4   2

This book is printed on acid-free paper. ∞

BOOK DESIGN BY DEBORAH KERNER

THIS BOOK IS DEDICATED TO MY GRANDMOTHER,
IDELLA JONES CHILDS, MY MOTHER, JEAN CHILDS YOUNG,
AND MY DAUGHTER, TAYLOR MARIE STANLEY.

"And what does the Lord require of you,
but to do justice, to love kindness
and to walk humbly with your God?"

MICAH 6:8

CONTENTS

FOREWORD

BY CORETTA SCOTT KING

This lovely book is at once a manual for living a meaningful life and a tribute to a wonderful, extraordinary woman who taught us all something about courage, service, dignity, and grace.

I was privileged to know Jean Childs since we were children growing up in Perry County, Alabama. We attended the same school, Lincoln Normal, where she was enrolled in the elementary school department, while I was a high school student. We were both destined to marry men who became national and international leaders and find ourselves close friends caught up in a movement that would change America and inspire nonviolent revolutions all over the world.

Jean's husband, the Reverend Andrew Young, served as one of my husband, Martin Luther King Jr.'s closest and most trusted aides in the Southern Christian Leadership Conference. Over the years we shared many common concerns, especially about the work of our husbands and the civil rights movement, and also the challenges we each faced in raising four children. When my husband was assassinated, I had to fly to Memphis to bring Martin home to Atlanta for his funeral and Jean was there to give my children comfort.

Later Jean would meet the challenges as the spouse of a congressman, Ambassador to the United Nations, and Mayor of Atlanta. As Andrew Young has said on many occasions, he was much blessed to have such a strong wife and exceptional mother for his children, as well as a true partner and coworker who shared his active commitment to the causes of racial justice, world peace, brotherhood, and sisterhood.

Even in the midst of such unrelenting demands on her time, Jean never relaxed her involvement on behalf of children's rights and so many important social change causes, always without the slightest interest in personal recognition. The King Center was blessed to have Jean's participation in our workshops and educational programs over the years, especially the "Celebrate Difference" program she helped to create and which educated thousands of children about the values of interracial cooperation, nonviolence, and love for all people.

Jean was truly an "earth mother" who worked selflessly for the health, development, education, and well-being of all children, a commitment which lead to her richly deserved appointment as U.S. Chair for the International Year of the Child.

Everyone who knew Jean Childs Young admired her for the energetic and tireless work ethic and the remarkable humility she brought to all of the great causes she championed. We all knew that she was a woman of exceptional wisdom, strength, and insight. Now, with the publication of this book by her daughter, Andrea Young, we have a moving witness to the beliefs, faith, and the beautiful soul of one of the civil rights movement's most vibrant, beloved, and dedicated women.

LIFE LESSONS
MY MOTHER
TAUGHT ME

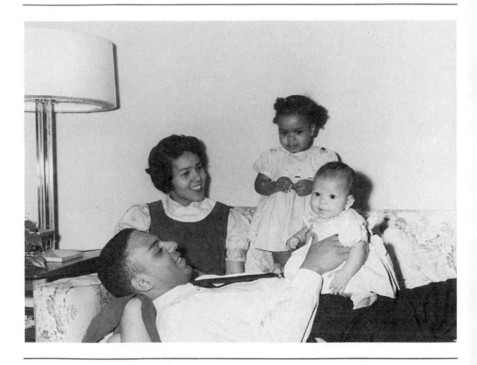

INTRODUCTION

Jimmy and Rosalynn Carter made their way down the wide, sterile hospital corridor, smiling and nodding at patients and nurses in a manner that, while gracious, discouraged further interaction. The manners so ingrained in black and white in the South inhibited anyone from slowing the Carters' progress toward their destination. One of the many loyal guardians who hovered in and around the room hurried inside to ensure that my mother was prepared to receive visitors. Her room was filled with flowers, enormous bouquets of exotic blooms and small pots of African violets which lined the windowsill, the shelves, and every flat surface of the room, and released a soothing scent that softened the sharp smells of the hospital.

Politely, the former president of the United States, in soft, south Georgia tones, asked permission to enter. "Hello, Jean," he said. "Rosalynn and I are on our way to the Sudan. But we didn't want to leave without seeing how you were doing." They spoke with my mother quietly and calmly, confident that their presence conveyed more than words.

In contrast to the Carters' understated, unassuming arrival, Jesse Jackson arrived at the hospital with a noisy entourage. He greeted everyone in the racially diverse staff, hugging nurses, pointing to people too far away to touch, offering the acknowledgment—"I see you." An assurance so important in black culture that in two major African languages—Zulu and Swahili—"I see you" is the literal translation of their words of greeting. For African-Americans, so often rendered invisible by their second-class status in America, recognition from a person of such stature was especially important. Jackson's expansiveness was culturally appropriate and necessary given his standing in America's black community. But even he quieted as he approached my mother's room. He entered alone, his expression grave. The politician part of Jackson fell away and the pastoral persona took control; he enfolded both of my mother's hands in his and began to pray, a rhythmic, emotional, Baptist prayer of the kind that makes blood tremor in the veins.

All summer, visitors had made their pilgrimage to the room on the fifth floor, the oncology floor of the Crawford Long Hospital of Emory University. Coretta Scott King; Maya Angelou; Billye and Hank Aaron; Ron Allen, the Chairman of Delta Airlines; Billy Payne, the President of the Atlanta Committee for the Olympic Games; Maynard Jackson, Atlanta's first black mayor. Teachers, clergy of various denominations, trade unionists, civil rights stalwarts, students, civil servants, people from every walk of life were visitors to the fifth floor.

Who was Jean Childs Young, my mother, a woman who received visits from former presidents and presidential candidates, mayors and members of Congress, corporate leaders and celebrities, and the parade of people from every sector of the Atlanta community? These people had come to honor the good wife of Andrew Young, former mayor of Atlanta and UN ambassador, friend and colleague of Martin Luther King, Jr. Andrew was a man recognized around the world for his efforts on behalf of justice and human rights and a key leader in the American civil rights movement.

The diverse group of women guarding Jean Young's door suggested that she was more than the wife of a well-known and well-respected leader. These were women with positions of influence in government, social-service organizations, and major corporations. They were members of Jean's own court, colleagues, co-conspirators, and members of her "standing committee of the house" who gathered regularly to plan events, fund-raisers, and demonstrations, more visibly on behalf of her husband, but more regularly on behalf of children and youth.

I was one of the guardians. During the last phase of my mother's battle with cancer, I was working as Chief of Staff to a member of Congress. I had repeatedly left Washington, D.C., to sit at my mother's bedside or stand outside her door to protect her and to greet the steady stream of visitors and the large family that maintained a vigil at the hospital. I simultaneously resented the intrusion and was amazed by the procession of people who found it necessary to come to her bedside and offer words of comfort. Their presence was a tribute to the quiet and powerful impact she had made during a life that would end too soon. I had always believed my mother could vanish pain with a kiss, and boost one's self-confidence with a steady gaze and a kind word. Standing in the hall outside the door of her hospital room, watching the parade of people passing within, the daily carts of flowers delivered there, I realized that hundreds, even thousands of other people believed it, too. My admiration for my mother was more than the remnant of a childhood dream; it was a truth shared by countless adults.

On June 7, 1994, we gathered to celebrate my parents' fortieth wedding anniversary. Our extended family—aunts and uncles, children and grandchildren, nieces and nephews, and many others related by love rather than blood—assembled in a private sitting room at the hospital. As I looked around the room I saw so many children: my daughter, my nieces and nephews, the small children of cousins. I though to myself, "How will they know her? What will they remember of their grandmother, their Aunt Jean?" I looked at my youngest sister, pregnant with a baby my mother would never hold in her arms. I knew that somehow I would have to find a way to share my mother's wisdom and her values with the next generation. Others needed to know her and I needed to keep her spirit alive in my own heart.

Beloved wife of a well-known husband, proud mother of four, faithful Christian, civic volunteer, my mother was a woman who defied the neat categories and stereotypes that attempt to define women as either feminist or traditional, homemaker or careerist; dependent wife or independent single. On her pine-paneled kitchen wall, below youthful photos of Andrew Young, Julian Bond, Martin King, and Bobby Kennedy and among many photos of her children at different ages, was a photo of herself, a laminated clipping from an *Essence* magazine article, "Jean, the Other Activist Named Young." The photo was a clue to my mother's perception of herself. She was an activist who committed her life to improving the welfare of children, wherever she found them. Unlike many activists, who care for people as abstract principles, but remain aloof from their own families, my mother included the care and nurturing of the children closest to her in that concern.

My mother was a woman of strong character, of deep and abiding commitments and a loving nature that drew people into her orbit. Her public persona was unflaggingly gracious. Married to a man who achieved worldwide prominence, she maintained her own strong individual identity. In the archetypes of Greek mythology, man is the bright, glowing sun and woman is the cool moon, reflecting the sun's light. That was the only pattern in the heavens that the Greeks could perceive. But, thanks to modern science, we are aware of binary star systems in which a pair of suns traverse the galaxy in tandem. Jean and Andrew Young were like a binary star system, each orbiting the other, moving together. When viewed from a distance, one star was seen. Those of us with a closer view saw the two suns in their complex pattern.

More often than not, the light of remarkable women goes unrecognized and unacknowledged. As the eldest daughter of Jean Childs Young, I feel an obligation to preserve the memory of her light. It is an obligation to her, to her descendants, and to myself. Throughout my life, my mother taught me many things about life, love, values, integrity, and faith. She was far from perfect, but her standards for herself and her loved ones were very high. She was my friend, my mentor, my guide, my critic, and my amen corner. In her home I could always find refuge and comfort. In her voice I found wisdom. Now that she has gone to her reward, I have found her voice within my own heart.

I also learned, standing by my mother's hospital door, the many ways in which her life touched the lives of other people. While I loved and admired her because she was my mother, there were many other people who depended on her love and her wisdom to give them direction in their own lives. I believe the things my mother taught me have meaning and relevance for everyone who is trying to live a good and purposeful life. As I search my heart and my memory, I share those lessons with you.

WEAR LIPSTICK

During her sixty-two years of life, my mother evolved from fresh-faced country girl to demure preacher's wife to harried young mother and schoolteacher to her final metamorphosis as a mature, confident, stylish woman at ease with any class of people anywhere in the world. She was flexible in response to external demands and expectations, while remaining faithful to the person she was inside.

Her unchanging rule of personal adornment was that she always wore lipstick. It symbolized my mother's development of her own personal style, one that fit her needs at each stage of her life. She taught me that it is important to project an appropriate image and is possible to achieve a balance between social conformity and personal preference. A woman does not sacrifice her integrity by doing so. Balance takes practice and the consequences of seeking the correct balance mean change over time—blue jeans are all right for students but not teachers. And, ultimately, the true person is more important than the external package.

Photos of my mother as a teenager in her small hometown of Marion, Alabama, reveal a lovely young woman in pigtails, a gingham shirt, and blue jeans. Although utilitarian in her own approach to clothing and ambivalent about her looks, from her earliest days Mother was exposed to women of genuine personal style. My great-grandmother had beautiful legs and wore high heels long after she might have retreated to more sensible shoes. My grandmother, Miss Idella Childs, was an accomplished seamstress and handmade nearly all of her family's clothing, including stylish, cinch-waisted suits for herself. As a result, Mother was accustomed to the comfort of perfectly fitted clothing and quality fabrics. Her sister Norma gained a tremendous appreciation for their mother's sewing talents and took advantage of Miss Idella's ability to make a fashion magazine outfit appear as if by magic on her daughter's back. As Norma grew to be nearly six feet tall and dreamed of becoming a model, Miss Idella continued to design and sew her clothing.

Unlike Norma, Mother preferred a cotton shirt and

slacks. Her penchant for simple clothes was reinforced at Manchester College, a strict Church of the Brethren school, where she wore the same crisp white blouses, full skirts, and white anklets as her classmates. Manchester was 180 degrees different from the quintessential "party school." The students were sober and diligent, and many came from farm families in the Midwest for whom college was a tremendous sacrifice. Dancing was forbidden for religious reasons, so instead of attending parties, the students gathered around a bonfire, snuggling and singing hymns and camp songs. Strength of character was valued more than glamour, and my mother's fresh-faced beauty and inner goodness were prized. She was voted May Queen, and for the school's annual May Queen dinner, Miss Idella made her daughter a taffeta gown. Though the dress was strapless, my mother managed to look shy and demure, with her pink lipstick and long hair gathered at the back of her neck. There was a bittersweet quality for my mother in her selection as May Queen. While she was pleased by the honor, she knew that it came in part because her white classmates saw her as exceptional. As one told her, "You are too pretty to be a Negro."

My mother's tan complexion and straight hair were a source of discomfort for her. She was fiercely proud of being an American of African descent, and she was insulted by any suggestion that she was attractive because she was lighter in skin than most other African-Americans. My mother saw beauty in those she loved—from the blue eyes and red hair of her college roommate, Dorothy Gall, to the rich mahogany skin and deep textured hair of her high school buddies, Esther and Princess, and the many shades in between. Mother firmly believed that beautiful women came in all colors and that the most important feature came from within.

It was probably under the influence of her fashion devotee sister Norma that Mother began her lifelong habit of wearing lipstick. She never left the house without it, not to dash to the grocery, not to pick up kids from the YMCA, not to play tennis. Norma, Mother, and my father toured Europe together in 1953, the summer before my parents married. Ever practical, my mother had lopped off her long hair to make it easier to care for. She signed up to go on a work camp in Eastern Europe sponsored by the Church of the Brethren. They could not be sure what conditions and amenities they would find in the camps or on the freighter that would take them to Europe. Later in Berlin, Norma was appalled when she saw Mother's haircut. She took Mother to her own hairdresser for a repair. A little lipstick, and Mother was ready to take on Europe.

It's difficult for us to imagine what a novelty it was in 1953 for three young American Negroes (as they were then called) to explore Europe—riding the trains, sampling restaurants and nightlife. Whenever possible they slept on the train to save money, and Norma remembers how people would do a double take when they saw my parents seated in a train compartment, hunched forward as they intently studied the chessboard between them. Norma spoke passable German, but in Italy the trio had to resort to more creative ways to make themselves understood. In a restaurant near the train station in Rome, unable to read the menus, Norma led the way into the kitchen and they pointed to the dishes they desired. "It's all in the way you carry yourself," Norma assured her youngest sister. At a time when Mother was not allowed to use the restrooms at the bus station on her travels between home and college, it was a revelation to watch Norma lift her chin and walk easily into the great museums of Rome and Florence, negotiate rooms in affordable hostels, and introduce the three to band members in hip nightclubs.

After my parents married and my father began to pastor a church in the small town of Thomasville, Georgia, Mother began to work out the balance between her personal preference for casual clothes and the social demands of her position as the pastor's wife. It was a trial-and-error process. She shocked the congregation of teachers and farmers by wearing sleeveless shirts and shorts in and around their tiny house. The Thomasville residents had never before seen a preacher's wife in shorts, and they found it a bit scandalous. But they approved of the simple shirtwaist dresses Mother wore on Sunday morning, and they forgave her missing hat. They also approved of her modest approach to makeup: a conservative application of lipstick.

When I was a young girl, Jacqueline Kennedy was the model of womanhood: the glamorous wife of our handsome young President and the devoted mother of their children. Not until Diana Spencer became Princess of Wales did another woman in public life combine those two ideals so successfully. In my child's eye, my mother was as glamorous as Jackie and Audrey Hepburn combined. She owned one precious cream-colored suit in the boxy style Jackie Kennedy made so popular, and she kept her hair short for many years after her European adventure. Her lipstick shade was a muted pink. Objectively, short hair was very practical for the mother of three active young children. She tended to wear pants, unless she was going to work or church, and even for church, she wore sensible heels and forwent hats and gloves.

I was a teenager when my mother began to adopt a more stylish and self-consciously fashionable approach to her appearance. It was fascinating to watch her calibration adjust to the new demands in her life. My father had decided to run for Congress, and my mother was faced with the challenge of presenting herself at community meetings, meet-the-candidate coffees, and wine-and-cheese receptions. One of the first major events they attended was a black-tie fund-raiser at the elegant Hotel Pierre on New York's Fifth Avenue. It was 1970 and flashy patterns and bold contrasting colors were all the rage, but Mother knew she could not afford a trendy dress in the newest fashion. She wore a simple princess-cut white dress with a train at the back, and she put up her hair and held up her head. She had no jewels to set off the dress. She put on a hot-pink lipstick and walked regally into a banquet hall with movie stars Harry Belafonte, Sidney Poitier, Alan King, and Lena Horne.

Organizing that dinner, my mother became close friends with her brother-in-law's new wife, Sonjia. Sonjia wore the latest styles and magnified her good looks with tremendous flair. She wanted to encourage Mother to do just a little more with her own beauty, but she didn't want to offend her sister-in-law. Finally, Mother asked Sonjia where she had her hair done. Enthusiastically, Sonjia made joint appointments for Mother and herself at the Scott Cole Salon in the prestigious Buckhead section of Atlanta. She and Scott encouraged Mother to cut her hair, which over the years had grown to a long braid that reached almost to her waist. Scott gave her a very modern cut, which set off the shape of her face. Thus encouraged, Sonjia began to introduce Mother to many possibilities inherent in shopping for clothes.

From that point, Mother's clothes and lipsticks became brighter and bolder. Mother's approach to clothing was naturally conservative, but if she was going to be under public scrutiny, she wanted to look good. The color videotape of television has a voracious appetite for visual images, and the fashionably bright colors of the seventies rendered the classic, understated look Mother had cultivated almost dowdy. Skirt lengths went up, electric blue supplanted navy, and burnt orange replaced taupe as major fashion colors. Mother maintained an amused detachment about clothes and makeup even as she changed to suit current styles. Clothes were not her issue. Her goal was to dress in a manner that was appropriate and get to her real work.

Looking through old family photo albums, the change in the fashion quotient in Mother's appearance is quite striking. After Daddy was elected to Congress, she became more stylish, even acquiring a regular hairdresser. Muted colors remained a feature of her wardrobe, but fashion colors were added—fuchsia was a particular favorite. By the time she went to New York during my father's service at the UN, she made a fashion column by buying boots at Bergdorf Goodman's tony Fifth Avenue store.

My mother was naturally attractive and she possessed an even greater beauty that radiated from within. She was a living example of "beauty is as beauty does." She wore lipstick and light makeup not as a mask, but as a nod to social custom. She was a grown woman and in the conservative South, grown women wore lipstick. She groomed herself to complement her social and political role and in her pragmatic way, she cheerfully acknowledged the need for conformity in those arenas.

Nevertheless, my mother did not allow herself to be defined by her clothes, makeup, and hairstyles. She was First Lady of Atlanta when Ron Lee, a talented but unknown black photographer, asked for her help in developing a series of photographs. A supporter of the arts, she enthusiastically agreed. Lee's concept was to photograph mature women, the character and complexity of their faces undiluted by makeup and other adornments. The series was titled, "Women with Wet Hair" and the exhibit was immediately controversial. A reviewer for the *Atlanta Constitution* all but demanded to know why the women in the pictures had agreed to be photographed in what she insisted were unflattering circumstances. She avowed that one of the women looked "deranged." A photograph of my mother accompanied the article. The reviewer conceded that Mother didn't look "too bad," but asked rhetorically whether she would want her grandchildren to see this picture.

The furor this exhibit aroused genuinely surprised Mother. She responded that she would be proud to have her grandchildren see the photograph, and indeed, when the exhibit was taken down she placed the photograph on a wall in her home. Today, I have it in mine. In the picture, Mother wears a kind of Mona Lisa smile. It is a reminder that behind the cultivated image, there is a flesh-and-blood woman with spirit and character.

Mother always assured me that I was beautiful without

makeup and shouldn't trouble myself about it. Though I experimented with cosmetics briefly as a preteen, makeup went out when my new feminist consciousness came in. This was the seventies and I was enamored of radical feminism and being authentically black. I wanted to be appreciated for my mind and my personality, and not my looks. To be black and a feminist in the seventies was to experience notions of beauty and appearance as a minefield. Chemically straightened hair was socially acceptable, but would it indicate self-hatred? I wore a large, Angela Davis–sized Afro—which, ironically, was only possible because I did not have purely African tight curly hair. In college, I wore dark-hued dashikis, black leotards, and jeans, and no makeup to speak of. At Swarthmore College, freedom of personal expression was accepted, even encouraged. Everyone was experimenting with the politics of identity. As women's studies and black studies were emerging as academic disciplines, we boycotted lettuce and fasted for world hunger.

It was probably my senior year in college when my mother looked at me with an appraising eye as I was headed for the door and pronounced, "Put on some lipstick." I hesitated, and she said firmly, "You need to wear lipstick." My intellectual exploration of sexual politics led me to view lipstick as roughly equivalent to a man's tie in the subconscious sexual language of the human species. But lipstick on a woman also suggested a certain level of maturity. My mother was simply letting me know that I was a grown woman, and as a minor concession to the realities of American culture it was time to wear lipstick. It did not improve my appearance so much as a little lipstick and some powder across a shiny nose "finished" it. Along with neat and clean, a little finish was appropriate. Mother in no way saw this as a major political statement.

When it was her turn, my sister Lisa received the same instruction: "Your lips look pale, put on some lipstick." Lisa protested that she wore Vaseline on her lips for a natural look. My mother commented in her dry way that the Vaseline made her mouth look like she'd been eating fried chicken. She needed some color.

My mother found my angst over these matters amusing. In her view, symbols of dress and makeup had no more power than we allowed them to have. From her vantage point, I was obsessing over symbols rather than the underlying reality. Her ingrained pragmatism meant that Mother focused on areas of central concern, not on peripheral issues. She thought the feminist focus on bras and makeup was distracting. For her, the real issues for women's equality had to do with money—with equal access to good jobs and equal pay for equal work.

Mother believed a woman had to develop her own personal style, but she could not ignore the basic language of adornment that was prevalent in her own culture. She knew that who we are is stronger than how we wear our clothes, makeup, and hair—that was the message in her Ron Lee photograph. But it is also true that clothes and makeup send messages in our culture and a wise person picks her battles. Unless one is choosing to fight for justice on the battlefield of adornment, personal style should be developed within a range of appropriate cultural cues.

It is not easy for women to do this. I am reminded of the magazine and newspaper articles over Vice-Presidential candidate Geraldine Ferraro's short-sleeved dresses and Hillary Clinton's hairbands. One of my mother's accomplishments as a woman in public life was that her clothes were unremarkable—neither stylish nor dowdy enough to merit comment. She managed to dress appropriately, even fashionably, and her style of dress never distracted from her purpose or message. Her clothes very intentionally did not make a statement, rather her words and actions made the statement. She believed, in effect, put on a skirted suit, a nice pair of Italian pumps, and a swipe of lipstick—then go out and change the world.

I spent several years rebelling against the culture of beauty, what Naomi Wolf termed "the Beauty Myth" in her book of the same name. My father joked that I could attend a formal dinner in jeans and a T-shirt when the invitation required black tie or national dress—jeans and a T-shirt being my national dress. When I was still in school I could indulge myself, because I had the luxury of not having to earn a living.

But when I finished law school, I had to change my approach to clothes, just as I had seen my mother do years earlier. My first job as a freshly minted attorney was representing poor people who had received the death penalty for their crimes. My focus was to represent my client and prevent his execution. My work took me into rural Southern courthouses where the marriage records were maintained in separate books for blacks and whites and the vestiges of segregated bathrooms and water fountains were still visible. As a woman and an African-American in a courthouse ruled by conservative Southerners, it would have been self-destructive to show up to represent my clients in jeans or a dashiki. I bought a blue-and-white-striped seersucker skirted suit from Brooks Brothers to wear as my summer uniform and a navy suit for winter.

Initially, I felt fairly ridiculous in a store like Brooks Brothers—going to the clothes closet of the establishment to dress for my very anti-establishment work. But I remembered my mother's example—the clothes were a means to an end, not an end in themselves. The goal was to dress appropriately and in a manner that did not attract any particular attention or distract from what I had come to do. It was important to my work to send the right signals.

As I have matured, I have come to deeply appreciate my mother's very practical approach to appearance and personal style. I continually experiment with the correct balance for my life and work. Like my mother, I married a minister and I had no aspiration of becoming the best-dressed woman in the congregation. A suit or dress and a string of pearls are my staples for Sunday best.

My experience has taught me that the transactions of daily life go more smoothly when I am well-dressed and well-groomed. When I am casually attired, I am rendered virtually invisible. It's difficult to get a taxi or the attention of a sales clerk. In contrast, when I am well-dressed, wearing a suit and heels and red lipstick, I find the world a much more responsive place.

My mother came to believe that it was fine to make the best of your looks, as long as you didn't allow it to become a preoccupation or a measure of your self-worth. It was worthwhile to dress in an appropriate manner, and in some settings a little glamour was called for. Mother learned to enjoy clothes, although she would always prefer slacks and a morning in her garden to a formal evening in a designer gown. If her responsibilities demanded that she attend such an event, her view was that she might as well look fabulous. And if she was just running to the mall, taking a brief moment to remove the shine from her nose and put on a little lipstick was, for her, more a symbol of self-regard than an attempt to impress others.

Today, the middle-aged equivalent of a T-shirt and jeans—khakis and a polo shirt—are still my favorite form of dress. Remembering my mother's admonition, I make it a point to wear lipstick if I'm leaving the house. When my daughter watches me refresh my lipstick just before leaving the house or getting out of the car, it's hard to explain the meaning of the ritual. She always tells me I don't need it. But it's not a mask and it's not that I don't think I am attractive without it. I can acknowledge that others judge appearance without measuring my own self-worth by how I look. True beauty comes from within, but a dash of lipstick complements it quite nicely.

A 50:50 MARRIAGE
WILL NOT WORK

***

My mother's wedding was a classic fifties fairy tale. She received an engagement ring at Christmas during her senior year in college, and she married my father in June, immediately after graduation. She wore a white dress that her mother had made, and she said her vows in a trim clapboard church with a steeple and bell. The bridesmaids wore blue. The groomsmen wore black.

A true innocent who married her first real boyfriend, my mother was also a strong-willed woman with deeply held beliefs about marriage and family. In her wedding vows, she promised "'til death do us part," a promise that she kept. And she promised to love, honor, and cherish, but not to obey. In order for a marriage to prosper, she believed, each partner had to give more than his or her share. In marriage, you gave all you had, not what was technically fair.

My mother's view of marriage was influenced by the relationships of those individuals closest to her. Her parents had known each other all of their lives and married despite some disapproval on the part of my grandfather's family. Although raised in a very respectable family, it was an open secret in my grandmother's small town that her birth was the result of an illicit relationship, and that the woman who raised her was not her biological mother, but her aunt. Despite the initial coldness of her husband's family, my grandmother was always more than gracious to them.

My grandfather's family had their own private scandal, in which the guilty party was my great-grandfather—Charles Sumner Childs. Charles married a gracious and gentle woman who was one of the first graduates of Talledega College, a college for black students founded after the Civil War by the American Missionary Association. But Charles lived openly with his mistress, a relationship that he either began or resumed almost as soon as his first son, my grandfather, was born.

The Childs men all worked in the family business—a bakery and grocery where they also sold their homemade candy. My grandfather, Norman, sold the candy to other stores throughout Alabama, traveling as far south as Mobile. My grandmother taught elementary school. When my grandfather was in his forties, his uncle, who was the head of the family, sold the business. His reasoning is lost to me, but it had a devastating impact on my grandmother and her family. Charles committed suicide, and my grandfather began to drink heavily.

Faced with a husband and family that was threatening to fall apart, my grandmother dug in her heels. She could have taken my mother and her sister, Cora, the two children who still remained at home, and moved to Chicago or Detroit, as had so many of her students as well as her husband's two brothers and his mother. But she was determined to help my grandfather through the crisis. My grandfather was a good, kind man who was reeling from the loss of his livelihood and even his identity. The family business on Washington Street was part of who he was. Norman was a Childs of Childs Bakery, and now the bakery and his father were lost to him. He had been his own family's breadwinner, who missed much of his children's childhood working hard from dawn until late at night, and traveling hundreds of miles to sell candy. Grandmother encouraged, nurtured, and supported until my grandfather got back on his feet. He tried selling insurance, but was unsuccessful. Then he bought into a shoe repair business with a friend and once again had a place of business on the town square. Where once his hands and nails had been immaculate, immersed in flour, sugar, and butter, they were now stained with black wax and shoe polish. But his dignity was restored, and the drinking stopped.

My mother learned that unconditional love can see a good man through terrible misfortune. She saw her own mother live out the meaning of her marriage vows, "in sickness and in health; for richer or for poorer." She experienced a powerful example of the true meaning of commitment.

Having witnessed her mother's heroic efforts to preserve her relationship, my mother approached her own marriage with stoicism and determination. Together she and my father faced many challenges, from living in the fishbowl of a small southern town to enduring the kind of intense criticism that surrounds anyone on the national stage. Throughout, my mother was the anchor of our family who accepted whatever life presented with humor and diligence. When Mother saw the tiny run-down parsonage in Thomasville, Georgia, where my father was sent as a new minister in 1955, she didn't complain, but rather set to work devising a plan to turn it into a home complete with the modern addition of an indoor toilet. When the Ku Klux Klan visited their home to intimidate my father into stopping his voter registration activity, Mother did not flinch. She urged him to stay the course.

After a few years in Thomasville, my father was called to the National Council of Churches in New York to serve as a minister in the youth division. Leaving a cozy community in

Thomasville where her home, her church, and the school where she taught were all in the same block, my mother went to New York City. This was a drastic change. In Thomasville, the children of church members were Mother's students at school, and colleagues at the school were fellow church members. My parents had been partners in virtually everything they did. My father had a flexible schedule that allowed him to be involved with child care, preparing meals, and making repairs around the parsonage. My mother and father might see each other frequently during the day, at lunch or while my mother supervised children on the school playground. Their family life and work life were intertwined. But, where once my father was a few steps away, after our move to New York he commuted from our home in Queens to the National Council offices in Manhattan.

The National Council of Churches, although a religious organization, was based on a very traditional male model of work. My father took the subway into the city, then often stayed late for a drink with colleagues to talk about the day's work. It was an exhilarating time for him and a lonely time for my mother, who was left behind in their two-story house in Queens with two children. To make it even more challenging, my father was traveling so much that my younger sister, just a baby when we moved to New York, would cry when he came home—he was almost a stranger to her. But my mother was determined to make the best of it. She befriended the richly diverse families on our block—black, Irish, and Puerto Rican. The kids of the neighborhood were always in our yard, as Mother used her gifts as an educator to make our house the most fun place to play. We joined the Congregational church in nearby St. Albans. Mother also took advantage of the City College system and went back to school to earn a master's degree in education.

Still, Mother was anxious to move back South. When the opportunity arose to go to Atlanta to enable my father to work with a new organization, the Southern Christian Leadership Conference, Mother supported it eagerly. For her, marriage was a partnership that benefited not simply the couple involved, but their larger family and community. She had not experienced that sense of purpose and contribution to community in New York. It was materially comfortable, yes, but she didn't have the sense of being needed in her community as she had in Thomasville.

The Southern Christian Leadership Conference (SCLC) was founded by a young minister, Martin Luther King, Jr., who had led a boycott to end racial segregation in public buses in Montgomery, Alabama. Dr. King's wife, Coretta Scott King, had grown up just outside of Marion, Alabama, and had graduated from the same high school, Lincoln School, as had my mother and her older siblings. In many ways, moving to Atlanta was a homecoming for my mother. Here was a chance to restore a sense of partnership and community, and through her marriage to make a difference in the lives of many people. She saw this as an opportunity to give. She didn't measure the sacrifice and wonder if, by relocating to follow her husband's career, she was giving more than her share.

A marriage is by definition intimate and personal. It often seemed to me that my mother was the giver in her marriage, the supportive spouse. The more my father traveled, the more Mother was left with responsibility for the care and feeding of children and the maintenance of the house. But even as a child I could see that she was very happy in her marriage. When my father was home, he would make a special effort to share the family duties. He would make a hot breakfast in the morning before we all left for school, do the grocery shopping, and fix small things that needed repair around the house. It was his way of acknowledging that Mother made it possible for him to work in the civil rights movement and still have the comfort of a home and family to return to. For my mother, the fact that my father agreed in principle that they were equal partners in marriage set him apart. He was grateful for her support and didn't expect that he was entitled to it.

Together, my parents were nurturing, playful, and affectionate. My mother often said that my father was more emotionally open, always wanting to talk things through. My mother was more pragmatic: you do what had to be done—there was no need to analyze. In Atlanta, their loving relationship made our home a warm, comfortable place and a magnet for many of the civil rights workers related to the SCLC. Good food and good conversation were always available at our small brick bungalow. And on the weekend, it didn't take much to persuade my father to put on a Harry Belafonte record and pull out the limbo pole. Belafonte was a strong supporter of the civil rights movement and his calypso music was very popular with movement workers.

As my family's oldest daughter, I was increasingly conscious of the long hours and hard work that my mother put in to sustain the life we enjoyed. Arlie Hochschild in *The Second Shift* addresses one aspect of my mother's role in her marriage. Despite having a job or career, married women with children continue to shoulder the major responsibility for child rearing and all that goes with it. This is where the woman is sure to be giving more than her share. While the prevailing situation for working mothers is not my ideal, I am glad my mother set an example based on reality. I had watched her work a full day as a teacher and come home to supervise homework and prepare dinner. Many of the clean-up chores fell to me—washing dishes, folding laundry. In high school, I volunteered to take more responsibility for dinner; after all, I got home from school before Mother returned from work.

I was raised in a home where there was constant talk about justice and equality. As an adult, I could not help but apply some of those principles to family life and marriage. When I was in college I read a lot of feminist theory about marriage. Women have proposed, and some have tried, a number of different strategies to have fulfilling marriages based on egalitarian principles. I once suggested to my mother that marriage contracts should be renewable every seven or ten years. We were in the kitchen preparing dinner and she smiled at me thoughtfully. She seemed to be reviewing every seventh year of her marriage and said, "I don't know if I would have wanted to renew the contract if it had been every seventh year. Some years are better than others." She went on to tell me that a marriage can't be sustained if the partners start keeping score. What value would you place on the amount of money and financial support one partner provided? How would you value the amount of emotional support a partner provided, or the worth of giving birth to the children and nurturing them, taking care of the household chores, paying the bills, creating fun and laughter in the home? Most of all, my mother said, a marriage couldn't survive if the partners nursed grudges. There had to be forgiveness. My parents talked with Jeanne and Arthur Ashe in preparation for their marriage, which was officiated by my father. Having herself shared a life with a man in the public eye, Mother told both of them that the three most important keys to a successful marriage were forgiveness, forgiveness, forgiveness. Whenever Arthur would see Mother after that, he would say, "Let's hear it for forgiveness."

It is relatively easy for a couple without children to have a marriage of equals. It's like being roommates with a joint checking account. Chores and responsibilities can be shared. The first year that I was married, I commuted between New York and Washington and took extended trips to Africa. My husband and I ate out as often as not. No structure or pattern was required in our home life. When I was away, we had long conversations on the phone. I experienced tremendous freedom and the security and warmth of a loving relationship. I was also secure in my own earning ability, not dependent on my husband.

Children vastly change that dynamic. Children require physical presence, constant personal attention, and reliable structure. Before I became pregnant, I thought it would be easy to share the responsibility of parenting. Once my daughter was born, however, I became very possessive. I wanted to do everything for her. When I decided to take time off from work to stay home with my baby, I was financially dependent on my husband for the first time. It was frightening. I believed that my personal attention was the best I could do for my small daughter, and I sacrificed my financial independence for it.

When I became a parent, I began to understand why my mother would usually talk about children when I asked her about marriage. Children are one of the great blessings of marriage and the best motivation to give that extra effort to have a strong marriage. But there is also a sense of working without a net. A woman with children is so much more vulnerable. Motherhood conjures in me the image of a band of hunter-gatherers moving through the rain forest to a new campsite. I often say to people that I don't believe in having more children than you can carry. They think I'm joking.

What I believe about feminism, now, is that it must be about choices. There is no one correct way for women to be in society. It is a sign of tremendous progress that women can choose careers that were once out of reach, but it is still unlikely that women with children will soon earn salaries comparable to their male counterparts. Married working women face high marginal tax rates and bear the full cost of Social Security and Medicare taxes. In our current tax system, married women who earn income comparable to their husbands pay higher taxes than do single-earner households with the same income. On the other hand, full-time homemakers have minimal income protection. In the event of divorce, a displaced homemaker may find herself with no long-term supporter claim to any retirement income. If a woman decides to have children, one very important factor in that decision is in the trustworthiness and economic viability of the man she chooses as their father. This sounds a bit coldhearted, but it's really very pragmatic.

In a family-law class taught by Judith Areen, now Dean of the Georgetown Law Center, I asked a convoluted question about protecting the interests of women who choose to be full-time homemakers and partners in their husband's career. I was thinking in particular about my own mother. How do we make laws and policies on taxes, Social Security, and pensions that take into account the complexities of families? How do we account for and reward the unpaid labor that women perform in the home and in child rearing? Areen had no real answer. As a society we give a lot of lip service to the importance of the family and the role of homemakers, but we give little to no financial support for those choices. In the midst of enormous progress, women have choices, but we bear all the consequences and costs of those choices.

The public policy discussions about this situation are very polarized. Conservatives propose individual retirement accounts for stay-at-home mothers. Liberals propose increased day-care subsidies and the Family Medical Leave Act. There may currently be a consensus opinion that the marriage tax on two-earner couples should be eliminated, but it still remains in force. These are all very modest, incremental proposals. There are no viable proposals to attempt to place value on the unpaid labor that takes place in the home. Bold thinking such as George McGovern's negative income tax proposal or universal child care are not even discussed anymore. While opportunities for women in the arena of paid employment have been transformed, the other half of the battle—making the workplace support quality family life—has yet to occur.

Given that reality, I am grateful for my mother's pragmatic example. In a world of imperfect choices, I chose to be married and have a child. My husband values and respects my career, as I value and respect his. He will buy groceries and cook dinner, pick up and take our daughter to school (so long as I keep up with the schedule), arrange for home repairs and outdoor maintenance, go to the cleaners and the bank, and handle the financial paperwork. He is very responsible about many of the tasks that promote home life. He and I share a belief that contradicts our principles of equality: we believe that for the time being his career is more important than mine. We both agree that one partner has to put the family first and most of the time I want that person to be me.

I reject the notion that only work generating immediate income is important work. I certainly don't want a return to the days when it was lawful to exclude women from a broad array of jobs; however, I don't think that enabling women to adopt a corporate, male model of work and career is the truest goal of feminism.

While we are striving for change and deciding what some of those changes might be, my mother's advice still pertains— a 50:50 marriage will not work. It does not operate on a balance sheet that is reconciled daily or quarterly. Sometimes you have to look at the balance over the lifetime of the marriage. Speaking informally with couples preparing for marriage, my parents always tried to help them understand that their relationship would shift over time. Partners grow and change and the marriage has to grow and change with them. Sometimes the partner who has previously been so strong becomes the one who needs all the support.

When it was discovered that my mother had cancer, it was my father's turn to give one hundred percent. He was unstinting in his devotion to her and in his efforts to obtain the best possible health care. He slept in a chair in her hospital room and when doctors in Atlanta could suggest no medical interventions, he found a doctor at Johns Hopkins Hospital in Baltimore to perform hope-giving surgery. He was steadfast in his attention. He was Mother's rock and anchor.

Together they had made their vows, and together they honored those vows. Neither kept scores or ledgers on transgressions and forgiveness. Each was able to count on the other for the love and support they needed for more than forty years.

RESISTANCE IS
A WAY OF LIFE

My mother was born in the Deep South at a time when the harsh rules of racial segregation governed the most common transactions of daily life. She refused to accept segregation, and with quiet determination she resisted the social philosophy that prevailed during her childhood—that by virtue of her birth as a female and black child, she was somehow inferior. Resistance was rooted in her abiding faith in a just God and in the American promise, "We hold these truths to be self-evident, that all men [and women] are created equal and endowed by their Creator with certain inalienable rights, among these life, liberty, and the pursuit of happiness."

The Childses of Marion owned their bakery and grocery store on the downtown square across from the courthouse. They owned their homes and sent their children to college. Mother's relatives were in the first class at Talledega College, her grandfather Charles Sumner was a graduate of Booker T. Washington's Tuskegee Institute. The Childs family did not fit the stereotype of blacks in the South before the civil rights movement of the 1960s—poor, uneducated farmworkers. They were industrious people whose ancestors, through hard work and good fortune, were able to use the window of opportunity that opened briefly during Reconstruction to escape many of the disadvantages imposed by centuries of slavery.

Throughout the South during Reconstruction, blacks lived and traveled freely. If they had the money for a hotel or first-class train ticket, it was honored. But, with the end of Reconstruction, the states of the former Confederacy began to enact laws mandating racial separation in public facilities. In the infamous decision handed down in *Plessy v. Ferguson*, the Supreme Court accepted the doctrine of "separate but equal" as constitutionally permissible.

By the time my mother was a girl in Marion, the forced separation of the races was more sharply delineated than when her great-grandfather came out of slavery. The Childses were educated property-owners who had lived in Marion for generations, and their accomplishments refuted the stated rationale for racial segregation—the supposed natural inferiority of

Negroes. Nevertheless, as Jim Crow took hold across the South, the restrictions were applied to them, as well.

Despite a legal system that relegated black Americans to second-class status, the Childses refused to allow themselves to be so defined. They would coexist with segregation, but they would not submit. The Childses had a long tradition of standing for justice and the aspirations to equality of Marion's black community. They were founders of the Lincoln School that provided a first-class education for its black students. Their children were raised to believe in their own worth and dignity and to resist segregation's demeaning message.

Even as a young girl, my mother engaged in a personal guerrilla war against segregation. The Childses' bakery sold the best cakes and candy in Marion, and some would say that no one has ever succeeded in making better peanut brittle. But ice cream was available only at the soda fountain in the drugstore. Mother loved ice cream, and she also longed to sit at the small tables with the heart-shaped–backed chairs in the front of the store. Negroes were allowed to purchase ice cream cones at the counter and walk outside to eat, but were not permitted to purchase ice cream sodas, since they had to be enjoyed while sitting at the tables. To add insult to injury, any white customer of any age would be served before a black customer, no matter how long the black customer had been waiting. From time to time, my mother would express her displeasure at these customs by going to the counter, waiting until the clerk finally turned to her to ask, "What do you want?" Then she would stick out her hand, show her empty palm and say, "Nothing," and walk out the door.

It must be said that my mother was encouraged in all of this by her feisty mother, Mrs. Idella Jones Childs. Miss Idella, as she was known throughout the black community of Marion, taught fifth grade to nearly every black youngster in town. She experienced a forced hiatus in her teaching career when she fended off sexual advances by the white superintendent, striking him with her pocketbook. Despite her excellence as a teacher, she was unable to return to teaching until he retired, since there were no sexual harassment laws in the 1940s. In my grandmother's case, she defended her personal integrity at the cost of her job—something she never regretted doing.

The daily flow of insults from the system of segregation would damage anyone's sense of self-worth. Virtually any occasion for interaction with whites required a strategy for protecting one's dignity. My grandmother earned extra money by sewing cocktail dresses for the students at Judson, a local private college for white women. When white adults came to the house asking for "Idella," my mother would bite back her retort, but if a young white person asked for "Idella," my mother would say firmly, "Do you mean Mrs. Childs?" This very simple reminder of common courtesy gave my mother a tremendous sense of accomplishment.

To safeguard their self-esteem, the Childs family boycotted most of the stores in Marion. For a time after their own store was sold, they drove thirty miles to Selma to buy groceries rather than patronize a white grocer who had insulted a family member. Martin Luther King, Jr., once said that no one can ride your back if you refuse to bend over, and Mother never allowed segregation to make her doubt herself, her abilities, her intelligence, or her character. The greatest danger of an oppressive system is that its victims come to internalize their oppression. By resisting segregation in countless, personal ways, my mother protected herself from internalizing a belief that separation was right.

As an activist—for racial justice, women's rights, or as an advocate for children—my mother was quietly determined, never shrill and unmannerly. She wrote her master's thesis at Queens College in 1961, replicating Swiss psychologist Jean Piaget's experiments in child development stages using her own children as subjects, as Piaget had used his. In her paper she wrote that her observations were comparable to Piaget's except in one respect. My mother found that her children progressed more quickly through the established stages. At a time when research labeled black children as disadvantaged, Mother was making a subtle point that it was their disadvantaged environment, rather than an innate inferiority, that was to blame. Her children displayed no developmental deficits, even exceeding the Piaget timetable. Her master's thesis was controversial because the sheer act of writing it undermined so many prejudices, as was her intention.

Over the years, my mother became an adept practitioner of creative nonviolence. Where possible, she refused to cooperate with the regime of racial segregation and supporting ideologies. In time, my mother would be in a position to contribute to a national movement that eliminated the mandatory separation of persons based on their race. The refusal of thousands of black Americans to internalize the inferiority implied by segregation allowed them to respond to the opportunity offered by the civil rights movement when the time came. When given the chance to use nonviolent direct action, picket segregated stores, and march for voting rights, Mother participated eagerly.

In her lifetime, my mother traveled to every continent except Antarctica. But her favorite trip had been in Alabama, where she walked in the hot sun, down Highway 80 from Selma to Montgomery to press for the passage of the Voting Rights Act. Our entire family marched the first day, over the Edmund Pettus Bridge, which had been the scene of an attack by Alabama law enforcement on unarmed demonstrators a few weeks before. I was very proud to be a part of that historic effort, although I was not yet ten years old. Mother then sent us children back to Marion to stay with her mother and she walked the next fifty miles with a core band of marchers. They slept in tents by the side of the road and were served dinners that were brought in by trucks. On the day they marched into Montgomery, one of the SCLC staff members found Mother and moved her to the front of the line of march. She walked proudly behind Ralph Bunche and Coretta Scott King. The march and Dr. King's powerful speech at the front of the Alabama State Capitol, once the capitol of the Confederacy, dramatized the need to guarantee the right to vote to all American citizens, regardless of race, creed, color, or national origin. On August 6, 1965, President Lyndon Johnson signed the Voting Rights Act.

Mother's commitment to justice was not restricted to issues of race. She was also an advocate for children and a voice for the rights of women. Freely identifying herself as a feminist, she worked for the passage of the equal rights amendment in Georgia and helped to elect women judges to the bench and other offices. In speeches she gave in the 1980s, she exhorted women to use the power that they have to transform this country, to make it a better place for children, for the poor, and for all women. This was also the time of the Reagan presidency, when there was a need for political advocacy against budget cuts hurting the poor and against the constant attacks on the civil rights measures protecting women.

In the fall of 1984, Geraldine Ferraro toured Georgia in her bid to become the first woman Vice President. At a rally downtown my mother was asked to introduce Ferraro. She spoke of Eleanor Roosevelt's visits to coal mines and poverty-ridden towns of Appalachia and rural America and the need to have that same kind of sensibility in the Vice President's office, honoring Ferraro with a comparison to one of the most admirable people of this century.

I like to think that Mother and I learned from each other with respect to gender equality. Having been brought up on a steady diet of justice and equality, I was deeply affected by the women's movement in the early 1970s. At fifteen, I discovered Germaine Greer's *The Female Eunuch*, wrote a paper on feminism in my social studies class, and began to read everything I could find on the subject. My concerns finally had a name—sexism—and even a movement—feminism. In my high school, relationships between boys and girls were excruciatingly traditional. There were many brilliant girls, but little feminist consciousness. There was a great deal of verbal sexual harassment, but it would be twenty years before anyone recognized it as such.

So I began my own experiments with gender equality. I stopped straightening my hair and wore it natural; I insisted on paying my own way on dates; I stopped wearing dresses, except to church. These were acts of resistance that I used to create space to develop my own individuality. I behaved contrary to expectation and observed the reactions. The first time I tried to kiss a boy instead of waiting for him to kiss me, he stood up and went home. And this was a boy I had been seeing for months.

As the family radical (which in my family was a pretty tough distinction to achieve), it was to me that my youngest sister Paula came when she wanted to play football at school. Her goal was quite modest; she simply wanted the girls to be allowed to play ball on the school field during recess. In the years before Title IX, the federal law that began to require gender equality in school sports, the privilege of playing ball during recess was reserved for boys under school rules. I encouraged Paula to start a petition among the girls at school and take it to the principal. Before long, Mother received a call from the principal of Peyton Forest Elementary School, asking if she was aware that her daughter was circulating a petition to let the girls play football during recess. Without missing a beat, Mother told her briskly, "Certainly I am aware of it, and we will be happy to supply the ball." So Paula won the day and the girls of Peyton Forest Elementary were allowed to play ball.

Racial segregation was the great barrier in my mother's life. It took tremendous courage and strength of will to resist segregation in the many small ways she did as a girl. She maintained a posture of resistance with no guarantee that the laws would change in her lifetime. By her example, she taught her children to believe that justice was possible and to have the fortitude of character to oppose injustice. She gave us a strategy for enduring oppression without internalizing it. When it was imprudent to openly protest unfair treatment, subtle resistance and noncooperation were always an option.

During my first year at Georgetown University Law Center, my property professor was a real bully. He yelled at students, criticized our answers, and had me very intimidated. But I was determined that I was not going to be frightened into silence in his class. One day, he proposed a situation to illustrate the concept of legal possession. I listened carefully as he described a customer at a grocery checkout counter purchasing beans. In a supermarket, the customer may have physical possession of an item but does not have legal possession until he or she has paid for it. "The beans are dropped," my teacher said. "In which direction are they going?" My hand shot up; I had the perfect answer. The professor called on me. "All over the floor," I said. The entire class roared with laughter, and I was no longer intimidated.

I went to law school to acquire skills that would allow me to fight injustice. I spent several years as an attorney in an anti-death penalty law group, the Team Defense Project. Mother, who believed that the state has no right to take a life, introduced me to the organization at a fund-raiser she hosted in New York.

One of our clients was a young man, Chris Burger, who had been seventeen at the time of a terrible murder to which he was a party. There was substantial evidence that Chris had been a neglected and abused child, that he had a very low IQ, and that he was under the influence of his codefendant during the tragic events. This evidence was not presented at his sentencing trial, and Chris Burger was sentenced to death. I left Team Defense while Chris's appeals were continuing and returned to help with his clemency hearing. My colleagues and I asked Mother to speak on his behalf as a child advocate at a clemency hearing. Despite the fact that she was quite ill at the time, she spoke eloquently to the Georgia Pardon and Parole Board about the injustice of killing children who kill. The clemency petition failed and sadly, Chris Burger was executed. Any time my siblings or I were resisting injustice, we knew our mother would be pleased and proud. It had never occurred to her that her status as the former first lady of Atlanta might be jeopardized by her defense for Chris Burger, a poor white boy from Indiana. The most pleasure she derived from her social and political prominence was using it to stand for justice.

Today, I am amazed at the freedom that characterizes my own daughter's life. Taylor is the first member of our family to be born and raised in a United States transformed by efforts to eliminate lawful discrimination based on race or gender. Unlike her mother and grandmother, she has never attended a segregated school or been denied access to a hotel or restaurant because of her race. She has never opened a newspaper to the want ads and seen columns for "Help Wanted—Male" or

"Help Wanted—Female." She is unlikely to hear a serious discussion of whether women in law school or medical school are taking spaces that belong to men. As she looks around for role models, she sees women and African-Americans in every possible career.

But Taylor must resist the temptation to believe that because injustice is such an insignificant part of her life, she need not be mindful of the needs of others. Her personal comfort may make her insensitive to the poverty and despair that crushes the hopes of so many. Fortunately, my daughter is a compassionate person. When we were downtown running errands a man asked me for money and I shook my head, no. Taylor asked me why I don't give money to the panhandlers on the street, which is a difficult question. Sometimes I do give money to strangers, I explained, but I primarily give money to provide food and clothing through our church. I believe this helps people more to give them direct assistance with the things they need in order to live than to give them cash that may be used for drugs or alcohol. Another day, a painfully thin young woman asked for money as we were entering a favorite West Indian restaurant to pick up dinner. Feeling guilty, I purchased an extra beef pattie. On my way out, I offered it to the woman who had just asked for money. "I won't give you money, but I'm happy to offer you some food." And I held out the bag as it had been given to me by the server. The woman refused it.

I make it a point to provide Taylor with activities where she can interact with children who are less privileged. The summer camp she attends has scholarships for a number of campers from low income neighborhoods in the inner city. Fortunately, our church is an economically diverse congregation providing an opportunity for friendships with young people from a variety of backgrounds.

My prayer is that we can see as much progress in the elimination of poverty in Taylor's lifetime as we have seen in the reduction of racial and gender discrimination during mine. Men and women of goodwill who have not been directly affected by racial or gender prejudice have still been essential to the changes that have occurred. Individuals like my daughter, who are not poor, will be essential in meeting the challenge of ending poverty in this most prosperous of nations. Ultimately, we are all linked. Martin Luther King, Jr., said it most eloquently: "Injustice anywhere is a threat to justice everywhere." As I learned from my mother's example, as long as injustice persists, it is our duty to resist it and to work for change.

PLAY TO WIN

Sports came naturally to my mother, and she was able to develop her abilities despite growing up in an era of limited athletic opportunity for women. She was proud to be known as a tomboy who rode motorcycles and climbed trees. In school, the only competitive sport for girls was basketball, so despite her five-foot-three height, she played and played fiercely.

Mother's team practiced on outdoor clay courts as did most of their competitors. Indoor courts were still a luxury not found in rural Alabama schools. The girls' basketball team played under girls' rules—six girls on the floor, two always on the defensive side of the court, two on the offensive side, and two who could run the length of the court. Mother was a runner. In a time when even men's basketball stressed ball control and setting up the perfect shot, Mother was a shooter.

Mother was also a good swimmer, despite her limited access to the water as a child. In Marion, the only public swimming pool was for whites only, so in the summer, my mother and her sisters and brothers would swim in a nearby creek. My uncles created a swimming hole by damming up part of the creek. It was dangerous for the careless: every summer someone would stray from the safety of the hole and be swept away by the main channel of the creek. But somehow in that muddy water, my mother learned to swim. Later in college, with proper instruction, she would earn a lifesaving badge. For her, it wasn't enough to be an adequate swimmer, she had to be a good swimmer, a strong swimmer.

My parents' courtship brought out the competitive spirit in my mother. As a seminary student, my father was assigned to the local Congregational church for the summer to organize and run a youth program. He had a room at Lincoln School, but took his meals with church parishioners. Before my mother had returned from her sophomore year at Manchester College, he had been a guest at her parents' home for dinner. Having heard so much about her, he was half in love before they actually met. When they were still getting to know each other, Andrew challenged my mother to what he thought would be a friendly game of table tennis and was quite startled when she fell behind in the game and announced, "No mere man beats me!" She began slamming the ball off the edge of the table in shots almost impossible to return. Her spirit only increased his interest in her. Himself a good athlete, he was already impressed by the fact that she had a lifesaving certificate. He met her table tennis challenge that day, and neither remembers who actually won that first game. Ultimately, it was a match they both won.

Mother continued to be physically active and competitive throughout her life. She surprised members of the Bethany Congregational Church, her and my father's first parish, by playing ball with the kids during vacation Bible school. The church was in the same block as the elementary school where my mother taught, and the playground had an outdoor basketball court. She and my father always played on opposite teams, and she was always determined her team would win. As often as not, that's just what happened. Mother was such a tremendous role model for the young girls in that small town so far south in Georgia it was almost in Florida. She played with the men and boys and beat them at their own game, yet she was a superb teacher, a loving mother and a good church-going Christian. She was a symbol of the possibilities in the world beyond the girls' quaint but segregated town: a symbol that a woman could take on challenges and barriers and win.

In her late thirties, when she was trying to get back into shape after the birth of her fourth child and only son, my mother took up a new sport—tennis. For the rest of her life she would be an enthusiastic player. Her new hobby came about after my father returned from a trip with a Congressional delegation to the InterAmerican Development Bank meeting in Jamaica. At the meeting, he noticed that a group of attendees, including Secretary of the Treasury George Shultz, had returned from a morning tennis match with the issues of the conference firmly resolved. Matters still undecided at the end of the formal meeting had been settled on the court. He decided that the next time there was an informal discussion on the tennis court, he would be there.

Together, my mother and father took tennis lessons, attended tennis camp with Vic Braden in California as their vacation, and practiced regularly with each other and other couples. My father became a good club player, but it was Mother who made the sport a regular part of her life. She and her sister-in-law, Sonjia, organized a team called the Love Ladies to join the American Lawn Tennis Association (ALTA) league in Atlanta. The women looked very dainty and feminine in their pink polo shirts and white tennis skirts. Together, this team began in the lowest skill group and worked its way up through several playing levels. It was inspirational to watch my mother play with women ten years younger than she was and use her natural speed and ability to place the ball precisely to win the match. During a match, Sonjia and Mother would use their break on the sidelines between sets to analyze the weaknesses of the other team. "Serve to the tall one's back-hand and drop volley the other one; we can beat these girls," Mother would say. Tennis is very much a contest of strategy, will, and mental toughness. If will and spirit were the deciding factor, Mother was unbeatable.

One particular match took place on Mother's Day. It was unseasonably hot for May, even in Georgia, and Mother and Sonjia were a little annoyed that matches had been scheduled on the holiday. Mother was so hot, after a fierce baseline rally she just lay down on the court. Her opponents were taking the match very seriously and began to quote the rule book on delay of game penalties. Mother got up and brushed off her skirt, with her eyes flashing. "I can't believe she's quoting the rule book on me," she exclaimed. "Let's get this over with so we can have Mother's Day dinner with our kids!" The other team was quickly dispatched.

My mother was a good athlete and a tough competitor who always believed she could win the match. But more important, she was never afraid to play. She was willing to take on a challenge and risk losing. She possessed the ability to win as often as not, but even if she hadn't, she felt that in a very real sense, playing *is* winning. Her tennis team would come together for the fellowship and joy of competition. But even if they lost, once a match was over, it was over. Mother didn't dissect a loss, or lecture or berate her teammates.

During a Congressional charity round-robin tournament, she and my father entered as a mixed-doubles team, although most of the teams were comprised of two men. Some of my father's Congressional colleagues teased him about entering the tournament with his wife as a partner. My parents played their way into the final, facing then Congressman George Bush and John Breaux, both regular tennis players and college varsity athletes. They didn't win, but Mother held her own, and the men were startled when she returned their tough serves with force and power. Mother was pleased with herself. She played to win, and she also knew how to define winning: when she met a challenge and gave her best. She didn't judge her play by the final score. At the same time, if she didn't play well, she wasn't satisfied, even if the score gave her a win. Mother relied on her own internal judge. She kept her own score.

One of my brother Bo's fondest memories is playing basketball with our mother after school. She would start dinner and then join him at the basketball goal in the backyard for a spirited game of one on one. As she showed him how to shoot a basket, make free throws, and master basic defensive techniques, they nurtured a strong emotional bond.

I have always enjoyed sports without being especially good at them. In the family genetic lottery, my sister and brother got the athletic ability, while I inherited the desire. My youngest sister won swimming medals in junior high, but later gave up the sport. I earned a junior lifesaving badge at the

YMCA, ran track, and competed successfully for the cheer-leading squad. It is almost embarrassing to admit that my best activity was cheerleading.

To make the cheering squad at Southwest High School in Atlanta, a girl was required to successfully perform several clapping and cheering routines as well as three gymnastics stunts—a cartwheel, a round-off and a handspring. I knew I could do this. I practiced on the front lawn for hours, failing repeatedly, getting up, and trying again.

Eventually, I could do a cartwheel with straight legs in a straight line, swing my legs around for a round-off, and finish a handspring without falling on my behind. I performed these skills in front of a panel of teachers and I won. It was my first real competition.

I enjoyed being a cheerleader. The squad members worked very hard at our routines and stunts, practicing before school every morning and even going to cheerleading camp at the University of Georgia. We had a leadership responsibility to promote school spirit and pride in our teams: both girls and boys. I was very proud the year our boys and girls basketball teams both won the state championship.

Nevertheless, I did want to find a sport in which I could excel. My mother had set the example that sports were good for girls. She expected us to participate in sports, though never pushed us to do so. I liked to run, but I wasn't very fast. I would have been more competitive at longer distances, but girls were not allowed to run cross country. The distance—just three miles—was considered too strenuous for girls. So I ran the 880 (half-mile). I never won, but I always finished the race. There were people in the stands who would jeer at runners coming in last. I learned to ignore them. On the track team, I was able to spend spring afternoons beneath a blue sky, expanding the capacity of my lungs to draw in fresh air. I pushed my body, felt my heart pump and my muscles strengthen. I was getting stronger and faster with every practice, with every meet. Wasn't that winning?

After high school, I didn't continue to run competitively, but I ran for my own satisfaction. I ran around tracks; I ran through parks; I ran through neighborhoods. One of my favorite runs is the loop from the Capitol to the Lincoln Memorial and back in Washington, D.C. To walk, run, or bike along the Potomac is also a real pleasure.

Despite my interest in competition, my access to sports was limited because I was a female. I completed high school just as Title IX was enacted, prohibiting discrimination against girls in sports, and I graduated from college long before Title IX was implemented. Girls were assigned the old gym, the old locker room. They had fewer coaches and teams. The football team in my high school had more school subsidized coaches than did all the girls sports combined. Where boys had varsity and junior varsity teams, girls had only varsity teams in basketball, softball, and track. College was not much better. At Swarthmore College, the women's gym was said to be the second oldest in the nation. It was scarcely large enough to play a full-court basketball game, with no room for spectators. The men, on the other hand, had an enormous field house with courts for basketball and indoor tennis, a rubber-surfaced track, weight rooms, and locker rooms adjacent to the playing fields.

I was mindful of those frustrating disparities when I had the opportunity to work on the preservation of Title IX as a legislative aide to Senator Edward Kennedy. Since the Supreme Court had narrowed the application of the civil rights laws, the Senate was crafting a bill to clarify Congressional intent and restore the application of prohibitions against discrimination in education on the basis of gender and race. Interestingly, opponents of civil rights measures were more willing to compromise on the issue of Title IX, gender equity in sports. Perhaps it had something to do with the fact that Senator Orrin Hatch, Chairman for the Labor and Human Resources Committee, had a daughter who was a competitive basketball player. This willingness to compromise was unexpected, since those colleges and universities who were the worst offenders attempted to justify the disparity in resources for men and women by arguing that football (an all-male sport) was an income-generating activity. Alumni of the big state universities warned all who would listen that Title IX would mean the end of college football.

As a result of Title IX, the opportunity for athletic competition for girls my daughter's age seems almost limitless. While still in elementary school, my daughter has played on soccer, basketball, and softball teams. She has had private lessons in swimming, lacrosse, and tennis. With my daughter, I apply the lessons learned from my mother's and my own experience with sports. Of the many options she can choose from, I have encouraged Taylor to find one activity in which she can truly excel. It is important, I believe, for her to have a competitive spirit and to learn to direct her energy and aggression in constructive ways. Right now, her softball team, for which she is catcher, hasn't lost a game in two seasons. Recently, the team was playing on an especially hot day against a team that kept coming back. The relief catcher was overcome with heat exhaustion and had to leave the game. Grumpily, my daughter went back in; she was hot and uncomfortable, but able to play. After the game she expressed anger over having to play when she was tired. I explained that endurance was part of being a good athlete and that she should be proud of herself for being able to come through for her team.

There are so many important lessons to learn through sports, including the power of being able to accept mistakes and recover from them quickly. When my daughter is on the field with her teammates—running, passing, kicking, catching—it is a good thing in itself, regardless of the final score.

Women need the physical, mental, and spiritual benefits

that derive from sports and athletic competition. Every study on women's health confirms the important benefits of regular exercise to reduce the risk of heart disease, obesity, and even cancer. Exercise has been shown to have a positive effect on depression, increasing the brain's production of endorphins, which are natural mood enhancers. Most important, given the stressful, consumer-driven society we inhabit, there is something spiritually calming and uplifting about taking a walk in the park, a run around a high school track at dawn, a stroll through one's neighborhood at sunset.

Unfortunately, most women do not exercise regularly, and I have often been among them. Younger women tend to focus more on thinness and not enough on fitness. We may not feel we deserve to appropriate to ourselves the time required for exercise. It seems indulgent to walk or run in the morning when the beds need making and a load of laundry could be tossed in the washing machine. It's even more self-indulgent, we think, to play on a team with evening practices and Saturday matches—taking more time from all those household chores that still fall disproportionately to women. It is an incredible challenge for women with children to juggle all the schedules—whether or not they also have paid employment—in order to create the space for exercise. Yet the benefits are so great: increased energy, improved ability to handle stress, the camaraderie of a team, the joy of friendly competition.

I have tried any number of approaches to regular exercise.

When I was single, I worked out regularly at a full-service athletic club. In the evenings after work, I would join a friend for a five-mile run. Instead of talking on the phone, we talked while we exercised. Once my daughter was born, running became more difficult. I took long walks with the stroller, and so walking became my activity of choice. The competition is with oneself—to walk longer and faster. Later, I played on a tennis team with a number of my women friends. Then the first year my daughter joined a soccer team, I found juggling the ever-changing schedules to be far too difficult and I turned again to walking.

The great thing about walking is that a pair of good shoes is all that's required. I walk with friends; I walk alone. I walk with my dog and beside my daughter as she rides her bike. I am an opportunistic walker: during lunch-break errands, I find that brisk walking and going a little out of my way is great for a short burst of energy and for relieving some of the stress of the morning. While on business trips, I walk around the area near the hotel. At one conference I attended, a group of women met early each morning to walk. The walking turned out to be a great source of information: it was networking as effective as my father's tennis play.

When I was still too young to baby-sit my younger sisters, my mother's exercise came mostly from working in the garden. She did virtually all her own yard work, planting, pruning, raking leaves, and using a manual mower to cut the grass. Mother preferred to pay for help cleaning the inside of the house, and to handle the outside chores herself. Working in the garden was good exercise; it got her out-of-doors and she found in it a spiritual calm, a sense of connectedness to the natural world. On April 4, 1968, the day Dr. Martin Luther King, Jr., was assassinated, Mother was planting a dogwood tree, a symbol of the Crucifixion in the Christian tradition. She was always grateful for the impulse that sent her into the garden that day. The spiritual strength she derived from her garden sustained her through the difficult weeks following Dr. King's death. She never again looked at that tree without remembering her husband's friend and colleague.

Women's bodies are meant to be strong, fit, and active. Witness the current boom in the popularity of women's sports. At the recent Atlanta Olympics, women's events were among the most popular: seats at the women's basketball games and gymnastics meets were sold out for every round of competition. The women's softball final was played before the largest crowd ever to watch a women's softball game. The popularity of women's basketball at the Olympics led to the creation of a women's professional league. I can't explain to my daughter why my eyes fill with tears when I watch a women's collegiate basketball team or women's World Cup soccer on television or watch Jackie Joyner-Kersey in one last Olympic competition. The strength and beauty emanating from these young women stirs admiration and a reminder that we can all play and compete successfully.

When we compete physically against another team, another athlete, or against our own personal measure, we win physical and spiritual benefits. When we experience our own strength, push our endurance, stretch a little farther, hit a little harder, as my mother taught me, it is a win for our health, for our fitness, for our own lives.

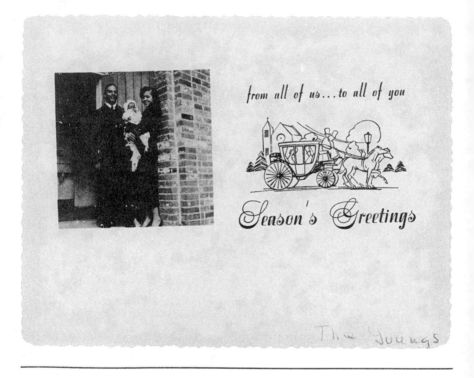

from all of us...to all of you

Season's Greetings

The Youngs

GO TO CHURCH

———————————

Looking through photographs of my childhood, one image that I see time and again is that of Mother with her three daughters dressed in their Sunday best. Over the years, Mother's hairstyle in the picture changes—long, short, pulled back, then long again. The dresses change and the three girls grow taller, but the consistent impression is that we were *always* just home from church.

This was an accurate impression—we really were! Mother taught Sunday school at the First Congregational Church of Atlanta. Every Sunday morning, she brushed tangled hair into camouflaging buns on three heads, gathered us into our family's dark-blue Ford Fairlane, and rushed to Sunday school. There we read Bible stories, memorized psalms, played with our friends, begged for ten cents to buy a soda before church, then went up the stairs to the dark-brown wooden pews of the sanctuary to hear the Reverend Doctor Homer C. McEwen preach. We were expected to sit in church with a certain amount of restraint and self-control.

The worship service was quiet and purposely dignified, with no shouting, heartfelt amens, or gospel music. It was oriented toward stimulating the intellect and calming one's emotions. The choir sang anthems from great European composers, and there was always a soloist from Morris Brown College, where our choir director was a professor, who blessed us with a classical rendition of one of the Spirituals. I didn't understand then the power and meaning of the Spirituals, but even as a child I was comforted by them.

In the children's choir we sang "Swing Low, Sweet Chariot" and "We Are Climbing Jacob's Ladder." We also sang "Climb Ev'ry Mountain" from *The Sound of Music* and "Impossible Dream" from *Man of La Mancha*. Each child had his or her own set of printed music sheets with royalties duly paid.

Sunday was a day for church and dinner; it was a day to praise God and to share a meal with one's extended family. Since my family lived in Georgia, in the fall Sunday was also a day for football. At the First Congregational Church, the Reverend Homer McEwen was ever conscious of the Falcon's home game schedule and was known to reassure his Trustees from the pulpit that he would not preach past kick-off. Football was perhaps already a competing religion, but when I was growing up, shopping had not become recreation. In Georgia, stores were closed on Sunday.

Reverend McEwen considered himself a scholar, and was proud of the fact that he had been awarded a doctorate for academic study. He had memorized all of the phrases in the traditional Congregational order of worship and recited his sentences in the service without using a text. "Bring ye all the tithes into the storehouse, that there may be meat in mine house, and prove me now herewith, saith the Lord of hosts, if I will not open you the windows of heaven, and pour you out such a blessing, that *there shall not be room enough to receive it.*" In the otherwise quiet service, his voice was the source of drama, along with the authentic pipe organ that played soothingly in the background during prayer and rose to a grand crescendo during classical anthems by Handel or Bach. Some considered our services boring, but to me they were like sitting in the shade beside a rippling brook—renewing and refreshing.

Mother never joined in the sniping about the pastor that tends to be as much a feature of small-town Southern churches as fried chicken suppers. She believed her role was to support the pastor and help his ministry be the best that an active congregation could make it. It was up to the worshiper to open her heart to the spiritual message of the service, rather than to intellectually evaluate the preacher's prose. She believed that one derived from church what one brought to it.

After Reverend McEwen retired, the church brought in a pastor who had a great deal of difficulty following in Reverend McEwen's footsteps. Then the new pastor began to undergo a tumultuous divorce. Our church was very traditional, and many church members wanted to take advantage of the pastor's personal difficulties to relieve him of his duties. An all-church meeting was called.

Although my mother had her reservations about this pastor, she had no doubt that it was wrong for the congregation to remove him for problems in his personal life. She felt it was cowardly and hypocritical, and she organized others to oppose the vote to fire him. She had no illusions about the pastor's ability to continue to serve the congregation; in fact her hope was that the minister would recognize he had lost the confidence of the congregation and move on of his own volition. Thanks to Mother's efforts, the vote to fire the pastor failed, by a narrow margin; he later left for another ministry. Mother's integrity would not allow her to stand by and watch a group claiming to be Christian behave in such an uncharitable manner.

Mother's Sunday dinner was a spiritual descendant of the Lord's Supper. She believed that the Lord was present wherever people gathered in His name. Her table was open to all who sought nourishment for the body or the spirit. Her generosity and hospitality were boundless; she welcomed the little children around the table as well as the stranger. She served chicken, lamb, or a sirloin-tip roast, but her signature dish was macaroni and cheese. It was a plain, solid food and the emphasis was on comfort rather than presentation. There were seldom enough matching place settings for all the guests, so some were served on the remnants of Mother's wedding china and silver while others ate from a Corning Ware pattern sold at the Colonial grocery store. If Mother was ever self-conscious about the fact that her table failed to conform to the standards of Amy Vanderbilt and other doyennes of etiquette, she never showed it.

Commitment to the Congregational Church as an institution was a family tradition. My grandmother Idella Childs presided over the tiny clapboard Congregational church in Marion, Alabama, with more care and constancy than any preacher the church ever called. The church looked as if it had been lifted from a village green in New England and set down among the one-story brick and frame homes occupied by members of Marion's black middle class. The church and the Reconstruction-era school that once accompanied it were the source of the education that made it possible for the descendants of slaves to live in modest comfort.

The high-pitched roof of the First Congregational Church of Marion was not high enough to make it cool during the summer, so Miss Idella would station a couple of fans at the front of the side aisles to circulate a small amount of air. It was a great honor to be chosen as the child who was permitted to enter the room off the entry where a thick, brown rope dangled and ring the bell for Sunday school. Whenever I visited my grandmother, I usually won the honor; I was the eldest of my siblings and I was a guest. While one was not quite at risk of being carried up to the tower by the thick rope, it was a little like riding a moving horse on a merry-go-round, rocking up and down to move the big bell. The deep ring would call from their nearby homes children who ambled distractedly toward the church, hair and clothing neatly pressed.

Miss Idella was superintendent of the Sunday school. She called the classes to order, and then divided them into two or three groups that met in different sections of the sanctuary. We children read our lessons, donated our small coins, and were dismissed until the afternoon, when a preacher would come to preside over the service of worship. If my mother was home on a Sunday with her three girls, she drew relatives and friends to Sunday dinner and the church service. Aunt Cora, Uncle Edward, and their three boys would drive over from Uniontown; Uncle Bill and Aunt Barbara came up from Tuskegee. Sunday was visiting day and anyone in the house when dinner was ready could expect to be invited to partake of Miss Idella's garden fresh vegetables, homemade biscuits, and pound-of-butter cake.

After dinner it was back to the church, which was even

hotter than it had been in the morning. This time the adults answered the call of the bell—ladies in flowered dresses and gentlemen in dark suits walked from nearby homes or emerged from staid Buick and Chevrolet sedans parked beneath the trees behind the church. The preacher was the last to come, parking his road-weary Cadillac on the front lawn and rushing inside, murmuring apologies to Miss Idella. Miss Idella handed over the Order of Worship, whispered final instructions to the Reverend Threadgill, and took her seat on the front right-hand pew. With her consent, the service could begin.

As long as I was living at home, church attendance was difficult to escape. In my teen years, Mother wouldn't force me to go to church, but sleeping in on Sunday morning was not an option. In her no-nonsense way, she would respond to my decision to stay home with a list of chores, including having dinner ready when the saints in my family returned. As a teen, I became very conscious of the contradiction inherent in our church. Jesus preached about caring for the poor, but our church comprised only very comfortable middle-class families. One Youth Sunday, the teenagers came to church in jeans to protest the dress code that we believed discouraged many people from feeling welcome in the Lord's house. The adults were amused and tolerant, but the formal dress code remained in force. I began to look at our church as lacking relevance to the world around me. It was conservative and quiet, while in the outside world there were protests against the war in Vietnam and middle-class black kids were imitating the berets and army fatigues of radical Black Power groups like the Black Panthers. Incongruously, in church we sang "fairer Lord Jesus" and our stained-glass Jesus was white with light brown hair as if our elders were oblivious to the "Black Is Beautiful" slogans of the day.

I drifted away from regular church attendance when I went away to college, but when I came home for the holidays, I still went to church with my mother. I became a Christmas-and-Easter Christian. It was an obligation, something I did to please others. For me, regular church attendance on Sunday was incompatible with regular parties on Saturday night. I chose the parties, placing a higher value on my social life than on my spiritual wholeness and well-being. But it was also true that churches don't quite know what to do with people who are neither children nor parents. For those of us who spent many years as neither a parent or a child, the institutions of traditional 1950s-style congregations didn't have much to offer.

When I began to sense a spiritual void in my life as an adult, I experimented with meditation centers and Eastern spirituality. I found the meditation techniques calming and centering, but I did not find the fulfillment that I knew growing up in church. The people who gathered for meditation didn't provide the sense of community I sought.

A worshiping community is like a village. In a world

where we regularly change jobs, homes, even spouses, a church community can be the one constant in our lives. It is a group that comes together at least once a week under a common bond of love of God and service to others. A church is organized to care for the spiritual and material needs of its members, and often of the larger community. There are groups established for the purpose of visiting the sick and feeding the poor. There are groups to which young mothers can belong in the nursery committee, groups of parents on the Board of Christian Education, ministries for singles, groups of retirees. Multi-generational groups assemble for the community's weddings, for the baptism of infants, for the confirmation and first communion of children, and for funerals—a reminder of the never-ending cycle of life. In such a community, one's life has context, meaning, and purpose. We are connected. We are members of a human society.

In a church community we are drawn to the true nature of individuals: class, social prominence, and career have less importance there than in American society in general. In fact, a church community often turns these standards upside down. The most respected church Deacon may be a cab driver by profession. The Sunday school teacher may be a former President of the United States. The most generous donor may be a domestic worker. The person washing dishes in the kitchen may be a millionaire. At its finest, a church community values its members by the service they perform.

A worshiping community gives us ways to act on our faith and our beliefs. While one can certainly feel the presence of God on the golf course, it is not the same as joining with hundreds of others to share Communion or a Passover supper. When we worship together, we intend to praise God and reflect on the moral and spiritual values by which we guide our lives. When we play golf on Sunday morning, we are more likely to reflect on the cost of our partner's new clubs than on the majesty of God's creation.

As a young lawyer working in the office of Senator Edward Kennedy in Washington, I enjoyed my work, but found the marble halls of the Capitol and Senate disorienting. It seems as if all of my colleagues were tall, slim, Ivy Leaguers who went skiing in the winter and rented houses at Virginia Beach in the summer. Senate staffers were all in good health and looked between twenty-five and thirty-five years old. This was not real life. When I shared my concerns with Mother, she urged me to go to church. There I would find genuine community with old people and children and people who were raising families on the kind of salaries that Senate staffers earned. Mother recommended a local Congregational Church, where the pastor was a friend of the family. His father had sent Daddy to his first church in Thomasville, where I was born.

I tried to avoid my heritage of staid Congregationalism and first visited more lively Baptist churches. But I did not feel at ease with the emotional tone of the services. Finally, I took my mother's advice and entered the dark red brick gothic structure that was the People's Congregational Church. Almost as soon as I sat in the pew and heard the melodies of the genuine pipe organ, I felt a sense of calm well-being. I looked around and there were older ladies in hats and little boys wearing their first suits. The cadences of the liturgy were comfortingly familiar. The senior minister's sermon was eloquent and thought provoking. I couldn't help noticing that he was rather attractive, but I put that thought out of my mind. At the conclusion of the service, I waited patiently in the receiving line and introduced myself as my parents' daughter.

I began to attend church regularly. There were members of the congregation who had attended Washington's Howard University with my father, my uncle, and even my grandfather. It was as if I had returned to my spiritual home. As spring approached, I was moved to really observe Lent as a time of spiritual centering, even slipping away from work for the midday Ash Wednesday service that marked the beginning of the forty-day period that culminates in Easter. Impressed by my faithfulness, the church's minister, Tony Stanley, decided to invite me to dinner. It had never been my intention to date a minister, but who could resist a courtship that was so mannerly and elegant?

As I write this, Tony and I have been married fourteen years. Throughout, the church community has been a source of strength and support. Scores of church members attended our wedding. When our daughter was christened, she was received by a community of faith that has been with her every day of her life. Members of the church are our friends and neighbors. In a metropolitan area of over 3 million people, our church is a village of 2,000 with whom we can observe the rituals that define our humanity.

I have cried at funerals and at weddings and applauded beautiful babies brought to the altar for dedication to God. The community of believers to which I belong observes the seasons of Christmas and the winter solstice, Easter and the rebirth of the earth that is spring; we bless our students and affirm our mothers and fathers. We care for the less fortunate members of our community. We share our praise of God and our common endeavor to live a faithful life. In this congregation I am connected to the mystery of life, the sense of God's purpose for us all.

LIVE YOUR OWN LIFE

When people would ask my father how he had stayed married to the same woman for so many years, he would reply with a puzzled expression, "She hasn't been the same woman." And he meant it. My mother was always growing and changing. Despite the increasing international fame of her husband, she was her own person. She always maintained her own identity and lived her own life.

Father's work as a leader of the Southern Christian Leadership Conference (SCLC) took him across the nation. In the 1960s, travel and communication were not as instantaneous as they are today. Most of the towns where civil rights campaigns took place—Albany, Birmingham, Selma—were best reached by car on an unfinished interstate system and old-fashioned U.S. highways. My father was away for weeks at a time.

My mother responded to this challenge by developing her own support system. Although she had no relatives or close friends in Atlanta when we moved there, when she began to teach in the public schools, her network expanded and she began a lifelong friendship with her colleague Sammy Bacote and his wife, Joyce.

Mother met Sammy one morning soon after she began to teach at Whitefoord Elementary School. After getting her three daughters up and ready for the day, breakfast served and hair combed, my father asked her to drop him at the airport. This made her late getting to work. It was raining, and she had been further delayed by rush-hour traffic coming into town. As was typical, Mother was carrying special lessons she had developed for her class and new books that she had ordered with her own funds. Dreading to face the school's principal, a stickler for punctuality, she slipped on the wet floor of the hallway and went sprawling. She dropped all of her lesson plans and papers, scattering them on the floor, and burst into tears of frustration and humiliation. Sammy Bacote came out of his classroom and helped her pick up the papers. In a calm voice, he soothed her frazzled nerves.

Sammy was a native Atlantan, a rising star in the school system, and his wife's family had been in Atlanta for generations. After school, Sammy worked in his mother-in-law's real estate business, managing an extensive network of rental property. Sammy had an answer to almost any of Mother's questions—from who was an affordable plumber to who else in the school system would support a phonics curriculum. He admired Mother's dedication and effectiveness as a teacher and my father's work with Martin Luther King. Before long, Sammy had informally added my parents' house to the list of properties he managed, troubleshooting and arranging for repairs. He and Joyce began to include Mother in the social activities of other young families in Atlanta.

My mother began teaching Sunday school at the First Congregational Church, and quickly impressed the families of black Atlanta's Old Guard with her faith, sincerity, and dependability. Through First Congregational she came to know the wives of black physicians, black Atlanta's business leaders, and the faculty of Atlanta University Center schools who were members of the small but prestigious congregation. Before the passage of the 1964 Civil Rights Act, Atlanta was a racially segregated city, and social relationships between blacks and whites were limited by law.

A very active supporter of my father's work with SCLC, my mother opened our home to civil rights workers needing food and/or shelter. But she also developed her own friends and activities independent of the SCLC family. Her career progressed with ever-increasing responsibility as she was promoted to master teacher for the federal Teacher Corps program and then as an assistant to the deputy superintendent, Edwin Thompson.

In time, my mother's ability to live her own life and cultivate her own network of friends and colleagues would prove helpful to my father's aspirations. In 1970 when my father decided to run for Congress from Atlanta's Fifth Congressional District, he was criticized as a carpetbagger, albeit from New Orleans. Paul and Carol Muldawer were among his first white supporters, and they held Father's first campaign coffee at the house Paul designed in the affluent Buckhead section of Atlanta. Paul was struck with how much my mother impressed their friends and neighbors, and he urged my father to get her more involved in the campaign. But my father told him, "If you want Jean involved, you will have to ask her yourself." At that time the role of the candidate's wife was still viewed in very traditional terms, but my mother was willing to play the supportive spouse who regularly attended campaign events.

Mother did not consider herself to be an especially outgoing person and she was surprised by the number of people who greeted her when she and my father campaigned together. At neighborhood picnics, summer block parties, and at bus stops, teenagers would walk up to her and say, "You remember me, Mrs. Young. You were my teacher." As they visited churches she would see colleagues from the school system seated among the deacons. Greeting my parents after the service, teachers would nod approvingly. "You're Jean Young's husband," they'd say to my father.

Campaigning brought out my mother's competitive spirit. She organized her network into a cadre of volunteers, "Women for Young." This was the first time a political campaign in Atlanta had made a special appeal to women voters. Teachers were one of the largest voting blocks in the city, and they were dependable voters. Mother reached out to the teachers she had worked with, the parents whose children she had taught, and to her fellow church members. She began to speak as a surrogate for the candidate, attending community meetings and forums.

My mother's campaign leadership put my father in a different light. Jean Young had picketed Rich's Department store to protest segregation; had been a volunteer in voter registration and the March of Dimes; was a superb and committed educator; and taught Sunday school at the First Congregational Church. Clearly, Jean Young's husband was no carpetbagger or Johnny-come-lately. Aided by my mother's dozen years of involvement with folks from virtually every walk of life, Father was able to shed the carpetbagger image and be seen as a leader of national stature who would be very effective as Atlanta's "errand boy in Congress." In 1972, he became the first African-American elected to Congress from the Deep South since Reconstruction.

When it was time for my father to begin his work in

Washington, my mother made her own decision about the family's future. She elected to stay in Atlanta, where she had developed her own life and identity. There were excellent reasons not to move—Washington was expensive for a family, my father would have to return to Atlanta frequently, and my mother had a terrific career opportunity there. Her boss and colleague, Dr. Edwin Thompson, had been tapped to be the first president of a newly established school: Atlanta Junior College. The first person he asked to join his staff was Jean Young.

As my father launched a new phase of his career in Washington, my mother launched a new college. Officially she was the reading and developmental specialist for the open-admissions college. But, in the first year she wrote school policies, interviewed and made recommendations on most of the faculty members that were hired, and worked closely with the president on virtually every aspect of the school's development. She played an essential role establishing the college's culture and spirit.

My mother was a forerunner of today's Congressional spouses, male and female, who have their own careers and choose not to disrupt their families with a move to Washington. At that time, Mother's choice was unusual. A *Washington Post* reporter asked her if she wasn't concerned about her husband being in a town where the ratio of women to men was 13 to 1. She shrugged and said coolly, "So someone else has 26."

In addition to creating her own identity through work, Mother maintained active friendships outside her marriage. She always took the time to enjoy herself, especially with her sister-in-law, Sonjia. On one occasion, my parents and my father's brother, Walter, and his wife, Sonjia, were returning to Atlanta from Washington, D.C. The flight was overbooked and the flight attendant offered round-trip tickets to anyone who would volunteer to take a later flight. Mother and Sonjia decided to volunteer and to use the tickets for a fun trip. They tried to persuade their husbands to give up their seats and take the free tickets, but the men declined. Later that year, Mother and Sonjia used their tickets for a five-day vacation in Panama, sans husbands and children.

In marriage, two people become one, and it is all too easy for that one to be the husband. Age-old tradition has it that the husband is the primary breadwinner and the head of the household, which is organized around his needs. But my parents shared the image of marriage described in Gibran's *The Prophet*, of two trees growing side by side, neither standing in the shadow of the other. My mother brought her strong and distinct personality to the marriage and she and my father truly complemented each other.

I responded to my mother's example by establishing my own life and career before I married and began a family. I completed college and law school, worked with the Team Defense Project opposing the death penalty, and was working in Washington as a legislative assistant to Senator Edward Kennedy when I met my future husband. Before we started our life together, I had several years of living by myself and meeting no one's expectations but my own. That time serves as a good benchmark for me now.

Before I married Tony, the most elusive value for me to find in a partner was an acceptance of my having my own life. The men I had dated wanted me to fit into their life. They didn't really value my career. But the man I married passed the ultimate test. Before our engagement Tony actually gave me the position announcement for Secretary for Africa for the United Church Board for World Ministries. The fall after we married, I started a new job in New York while his work was in Washington, D.C. For the first two years of our marriage, I took the train to New York on Monday morning and came home Friday night. My responsibilities took me on extended trips to Africa and shorter trips to churches and church conferences around the United States. There could have been no more powerful indication for me that marriage to Tony would not be a struggle to protect my own identity.

My husband has always been very proud of my work and supportive of my many activities. It could easily have been quite different. The role of pastor's wife can easily become a full-time job. If Tony expected me to attend all his parishioners' weddings and funerals, attend every worship service during the week, and chair the Christian education committee and the women's fellowship committee, I would have had no time for my own career and scarcely time to be a good mother. As it is, I am a nontraditional pastor's wife. I am an active church member, as I would be because of my upbringing. I attend those weddings and funerals that I would attend even if my husband was not the pastor. I took a turn at chairing the women's fellowship, teaching Sunday school, and volunteering in the nursery.

Like my mother and father, Tony and I make a great team. One of our best efforts involved the visit of Bishop Desmond Tutu to Washington. I was working with the Washington office of the United Church of Christ and there was an opportunity to have Bishop Tutu preach for a special service for UCC churches in the area. Tony was happy to agree to host the event, so together we organized all the churches in the Potomac Association. I persuaded the Treasurer of the UCC's World Board to accept contributions on behalf of Bishop Tutu. Tony arranged for closed-circuit television so that the fellowship hall and chapel could be used once the main sanctuary was full. He offered a limousine-driver friend the honor of providing transportation for the Bishop. Bishop Tutu emerged from the car to an enthusiastic crowd that filled the church. He commented, "I wish the people back home could see how you treat me." In one event Tony and I together raised more than $30,000 for Bishop Tutu's anti-apartheid efforts.

During our fourteen years of marriage, Tony has never

failed to be supportive of my career. He has described himself as a great "horseholder" and has accompanied me to meetings and events where I was the featured speaker. When I was employed by an agency that held working retreats on Cape Cod, he would come to the Cape and take our daughter to the beach while I was in meetings. When I travel out of town or work late into the evening, it is my daughter who is more likely to complain. When I have a new challenge or opportunity, Tony's typical comment is, "Go for it." When I worked at National Planned Parenthood, in metropolitan D.C., he hosted a breakfast meeting for ministers to introduce them to a program to help churches play a role in preventing teen pregnancy.

Being a minister is an all-consuming job. My husband is often asked to visit families in crisis until late in the night. He gets calls at the early hours of the morning from families who have lost a loved one. Since his Sundays begin at four A.M. as he puts the final touches on his sermon, and don't end until in the middle of the afternoon, he is seldom available for socializing on Saturday nights. When I at one time found myself depending on him exclusively for social time, I experienced a great deal of loneliness. He was often physically present, but unavailable for conversation. He would be totally absorbed in working on a sermon or taking one phone call after another from parishioners. While I didn't have a problem leading my professional life, I realized then that I also needed to have my own social life.

Following my mother's example, I developed hobbies and activities for myself. Given the frantic pace of daily lives, it can be a real pleasure to sit with a friend in her kitchen and have a cup of coffee or a glass of wine while our daughters play. I have women friends whom I meet for lunch, or take an afternoon with to explore antique shops or museum exhibits.

I have had wonderfully, giddy times with my sisters. One evening when we were visiting Atlanta, Lisa and I left my daughter and her son with Mother and went to the Six Flags amusement park. We raced from one roller coaster to another, riding as many as we could before the park closed. We screamed off the weight of responsibility we felt as adults and enjoyed feeling like carefree, young girls for a few hours.

Still, there are some social events that I insist my husband attend. Once a year, a mothers' group to which I belong hosts an evening cabaret as a fund-raiser for a local charity. Most of us are working mothers who are either in a weekday uniform, the business suit, or our weekend uniform, the jogging suit, as we run from one chore and errand to another, shuttling children and groceries. Our annual fund-raiser is a chance to put on a cocktail dress and indulge in feeling glamorous and attractive. As it's on Saturday night, my husband always frets about attending, but once he is there, he has a great time.

Together, Tony and I have a rich, full marriage. We are constantly managing the challenge of living our own lives without living totally separate lives. Given our demanding careers, it is possible to find that we see each other primarily to exchange household or child-care information. There have been times that I seemed to see my husband as we passed each other on the walkway leading to the front door—going in opposite directions. Achieving balance requires good communication.

As my mother taught me, in life and in relationships we need, ultimately, to be responsible for our own happiness. We cannot expect or insist that any one person fulfill all our needs. The more you bring to a relationship the more you will get out of that relationship. Who could be less interesting than a partner without opinions, with no view of his own, no experiences that are different from your experiences? Independence may cause conflict and tension in relationships, but it is far better than being a doormat or cipher.

Living her own life, my mother brought so much more to her partnership with my father. Her sphere of influence contributed in no small measure to his success, and it allowed each of them to accomplish their goals to improve the well-being of the Atlanta community. Because they worked apart, they were also able to contribute more when they worked together. Mother was always her own person with her own vision of what she wanted from life.

CHILDREN FIRST

In all her actions, my mother was first and foremost an advocate for children—her own and the children of others. She believed in the importance of children, in their full membership in our society, and she demonstrated that belief at every level. She permitted her children to be seen *and* heard.

During my childhood in Atlanta in the midst of the civil rights movement, the door to our home was always open. Another place at the table could always be set for the many activists who made the movement possible: everyone from itinerant students to Dr. Martin Luther King, Jr., himself were welcome guests in our home. Mother had a magic macaroni casserole that seemed to go all the way around the table, no matter how many people were squeezed in. People had better manners in those days; no one would dream of taking more than his share, no matter how hungry he might be. No one would take seconds before all had been served. No one would ask for anything that hadn't been offered at the table. Proper manners, or good home training, as we would say, made sharing a meal possible when, really, there wasn't enough.

No matter how crowded the table, my mother never asked her children to leave it to make way for adults. We sat at the table—which, we had just helped to set—and we were free to speak. The conversation was dynamic and passionate, although my father was always a calm and cool presence. These men and women involved with the civil rights movement vibrated with hope and a belief that they could accomplish a transformation of society. It was exciting to watch Southern Christian Leadership Conference staff member Dorothy Cotton's eye flash as she described a voter education workshop, and to hear the trill of her laughter. The students at our table were so earnest and serious about their mission in the South working among disenfranchised sharecroppers.

Along with Mother's macaroni and cheese I ingested a conviction that it is not enough in life to find a safe place for oneself. All of these people at our table were educated and smart. Any of them could have carved out a safe, middle-class life and abandoned the black poor in the rural South. The same was true of my parents. They had left an integrated suburb in New York to return to the South to fight segregation. They had achieved the American Dream for themselves, but they were committed to working to make it come true for others.

At these meals, I laughed at the stories, expressed sympathy over the risks, and asked questions when I could get a word in edgewise. I cherished the opportunity to listen to the conversation, because I saw that in other homes children were banished to the kitchen when adults discussed serious matters. In fact, this was a time when in many black households, girls and women never sat down while there were men to be fed. Women served and the smart ones ate by tasting from the pots while they cooked, but many ate only after they had urged the men to consume as much as they could possibly hold despite the possibility that it might mean few leftovers for the women. Then again, maybe that's why running out of food is a cardinal sin among black hostesses; it meant the cooks went hungry. In a platter of fried chicken, the wings and back have very little meat. I have vivid memories of women in the kitchen after a lavish meal, picking meat from chicken wings. Among black women I know today, it is seldom the case that men are served first. Of course, guests are served first regardless of gender, and hostesses continue to serve at least twice as much food as anyone could possibly eat.

It was one thing to seat one's daughters around the table

during and in the midst of the informality of the anti-establishment civil rights movement, but Mother never backed away from that practice even in the most formal settings. When President Jimmy Carter appointed my father to be the U.S. Ambassador to the United Nations, our family was ensconced in the formal rooms of the Waldorf-Astoria Towers on Park Avenue in Manhattan. From the previous Ambassador, we inherited a French couple to tend to our needs. Diplomatic entertaining had established rituals that attempted to emulate the purported style of nineteenth-century European nobility. French cuisine and multiple courses, with a different wine and formal place settings with china and silverware for each stage of the meal, were the standard.

My mother refused to be intimidated by the formality of the official Ambassador's residence at the Waldorf-Astoria. During her initial tour, she calmly and critically viewed the enormous drawing room with its two seating areas and grand piano, the lavish master bedroom suite with his and her bathrooms, the dining room that seated twenty-four at one polished mahogany table. She frowned at the tiny kitchen and smiled only when she saw the sitting room where her family could gather comfortably. She pronounced the elegant living quarters "adequate." By that she meant that however suitable it was for formal diplomatic receptions, the residence at the Waldorf was barely acceptable for her two youngest children—an active four-year old and a sociable teenager. In her home, the needs of the children were paramount.

Mother took an unexpected approach to diplomatic entertaining as well. When my mother was the hostess, her children were invited, whether it was a small luncheon, a five-course sit-down dinner, or a massive reception. In this way, I broke bread with Joshua Nkomo and Robert Mugabe, now Prime Minister of Zimbabwe, as I had once shared a table with Martin Luther King. By this time, I was a law student and well accustomed to public life and the entertaining that accompanied it. It was both a pleasure and a burden. After a few hours of a very formal event, it was always a relief to retreat to my room with a favorite book. But if there was real conversation going on about political events, I was content to sit and listen until the last guests went home. I was always very conscious of my behavior at these events. While my parents were inclusive of children, I could sense disapproval from other adults. I felt a responsibility to be a credit to my parents. When my own daughter was young and portable, I took her everywhere. As she grew older, she would resist any event that required a dress. Recalling the pressure that accompanies the opportunity to attend formal dinners, I usually defer to her feelings about such occasions. I will persuade her to participate when I believe there is something for her to learn from, for example, a dinner honoring her grandfather. At home our entertaining tends to include other families, and dinner is always family style with children at the table together with the adults. I like the idea of formal dinner parties at home, but I can't imagine putting a lot of effort into a party that my daughter wouldn't enjoy.

President Jimmy Carter appointed my mother chairperson of the United States Commission on the International Year of the Child, with a mandate to develop, with minimal funding, a meaningful observance of the International Year of the Child. Essentially, the effect of the executive order gave federal agencies permission to do whatever Mother could persuade them to do—such as sharing with the Commission their staff, office space, and supplies. Mother acquired office space at the UN Mission, put together a small staff, and began to lobby Congress for funding for American observance of the International Year of the Child.

She promoted the IYC in every state and territory of the U.S. Her staff held hearings on Indian reservations, in migrant camps and in inner cities. She encouraged state programs (one of the state chairs was Hillary Rodham Clinton, wife of the young governor of Arkansas), encouraged coalitions, and drew attention to the needs of children at home and around the world. The closing statement of the Commission's report to President Carter reflected my mother's view of the importance of children:

"Over sixty million strong—one-third of America's

population—children are the adults, the citizens of tomorrow. Five years from now, ten years from now, these children will vote or not vote, they will be productive working members of society or they will lack the necessary skills, opportunities, and supports to make a decent life for themselves. They will be equipped to cope with an increasingly complex, technological society or they will not. They will be well educated, independent, informed citizens, or they will be functionally illiterate, malleable, and easily led. The choice is ours and theirs. We make that choice by design or default, but either way we will reap the results."

Whether at home or in the public policy arena, my mother's concern for children was the principle underlying her actions. She believed that a household or society that protected and nurtured the needs of children would be vital and strong, that a family or society that failed to nurture and cultivate its children had no future.

Today it is fashionable to say that it takes a village to raise a child, but the status of children in this country has continued to deteriorate relative to other groups. Recent years have seen a rise in antisocial behavior by young people. We are no longer shocked by the tender age of some violent offenders. We witness the tragedy of students coming to school with guns and shooting classmates and teachers. When I read about events, I wonder about the parents and I wonder about a society that produces children capable of such crimes.

In an urban and industrial society (absent child labor), the productive capacity of children ceases to benefit the family of origin. An American child consumes family resources with no means to replenish them. Modern American families must cherish children for their own sake, with no expectation of reward. The benefits of the well-brought-up child will accrue to the society as a whole, not simply to his or her parents. The child who becomes a caring citizen, who volunteers as a Boy Scout or Girl Scout leader; who raises money for the local PTA; coaches a soccer team; visits sick and shut-in church members—this type of person improves the lives of many people who never changed his or her diaper or paid school tuition. Conversely, the dangers of the neglected child who grows up to be physically violent, who steals or abuses drugs, will diminish the lives of many people outside his or her family. In our tightly knit, interdependent world, it is increasingly difficult for someone to self-destruct without taking others with him.

In contrast, in a farm-based economy, children help generate wealth. Around the globe, children raised on subsistence farms begin to take on essential chores by the age of three. In that context, children have an intrinsic value, and are socialized out of immediate economic necessity. This was true in the United States as recently as World War II, when we began the transformation into an urban and industrial nation. When families leave the land, children cease to be an economic asset.

This is why in developing countries we see landless poor families selling their children to sweatshops, and in the United States we see children abandoned and neglected. The values and work ethic of the farm-based family are American totems, but we lack the political will to create the economic context to sustain the viability of family farms. Our leaders chastise nations such as France and Japan when they do so.

There is a philosophical battle in American politics about the rights of parents in contrast to the rights of the state. Many of our deeply held beliefs about the rights of parents are more suited to an agrarian economy of one-room school houses than to a complex, post-industrial economy where schools and office buildings contain hundreds and thousands of people. Contemporary culture wars over support for public education and government subsidies for childcare and welfare reform reflect a tension between the self-sufficiency and independence of our rural, farm-based past and our urbanized present, although different camps define the conflict as traditional values vs. liberal values. Among proponents of individualism and tradition, there is fierce resistance to the notion that the general society has both a need and a responsibility to ensure a basic level of support and socialization for our children and families.

At the same time, the ranks of the poor in America are populated with young children and their parents. Impoverished children are educated in the poorest schools, especially in our urban areas. Quality child care for working parents, after-school programs, and public recreation facilities are scarce where the need is greatest. Even middle-class parents find themselves in a time crunch—possessing the money to provide for their children's material needs, but lacking the time to engage their children's emotional and spiritual needs.

Parenthood is a humbling experience. The challenge of raising one small girl has brought me to my knees many times. Concerned parents are bombarded by competing messages: nature vs. nurture; multiple intelligences; emotional quotient vs. intelligence quotient; assertive vs. permissive discipline, to name a few. Parents looking for answers will find a bewildering array of theories available in the private arena, but essentially they fend for themselves. Unless they endanger the life of their child, adults are generally left alone to parent effectively or poorly.

Mother was an educator who raised three daughters and a son and took responsibility for every child that crossed her path, not simply those she bore. Her service as the United States chairperson of the International Year of the Child was one of her proudest achievements. She saw it as an extension of her work in the classroom, an opportunity to improve the lives of millions of children rather than just thirty at a time.

Mother put her own children first in her daily life. She loved to take her three daughters to church in pretty matching dresses, but she invested little in her own clothes. I recall that one of the dresses she frequently wore was nylon and came in a plastic tube. It had a rich, purple pattern and to my childish eyes she looked beautiful in it, but it was very inexpensive. She was very matter-of-fact about wearing hand-me-downs. In the 1960s she could feed a family of five with $30 a week, did most of her yard work herself, and was generally very frugal. Yet the local teenagers remarked how generous she was in her compensation of baby-sitters. As a result, we had our pick: Sandra, who was a lot of fun, but would make me wash the dishes as I was supposed to; Evelyn, who would wash the dishes herself, but made us go to bed on time; or Laverne, who would let us stay up late watching television, but chose the programs she liked. "You mother pays good money to keep her children," they would say. Mother had her priorities.

This is an example I follow today. A teenager baby-sitting my daughter for the evening will make at least as much money as she would if she spent the evening flipping hamburgers.

Adapting her own career to the needs of her family was another way my mother put her children first. She completed her master's degree while raising two children under five and one on the way. It was a race down to the wire to complete her dissertation before her third child was born. Somehow she managed.

It goes without saying there's no such thing as a mother who doesn't work. Mother moved in and out of the paid work-force during her lifetime, with the birth of her children and the family's geographical relocations. Her longest tenure was with the Atlanta public schools, where she excelled as an educator. She quickly became a mentor teacher in the Teacher Corps, an initiative of President Lyndon Johnson's War on Poverty, and later she became a curriculum specialist. No matter what the other demands on her time and attention, Mother's children were never neglected. Even when her paid or volunteer work took her out in the evening, we were assured of a hot meal and we were always conscious of the need to complete our homework to her satisfaction.

As a teenager and then as a young professional, I couldn't understand the sacrifices my mother made for her children—leaving a job she loved to move to New York with her husband; accepting supporting positions rather than going after the top job. I couldn't understand how she managed to work outside the home while raising four children. When I asked her, she would seem puzzled. "I just did what I had to do," she'd say.

Only when my own daughter was born did I begin to understand that a child could be a source of pure joy. The feeling a runner gets when she's in the zone, the feeling a lawyer gets when the Supreme Court takes her case, the feeling one gets in meditation—that's the kind of feeling that rushes through me sometimes when I look at my daughter. When she was first born, my husband would caution me—"worship the Giver, not the gift." But the gift was so glorious and such perfect evidence of the greatness of the Creator, our Father/Mother God. If we know the tree by its fruit, surely we know the Giver by the gift.

After Taylor was born, I adjusted my career to the demands of parenting. Despite my love of international affairs, I have limited my work to positions that don't require extensive travel. I have tried to balance the need for intellectually satisfying work with my need and desire to be an attentive parent.

Even so, I find I must struggle to be fully present to my beloved daughter. It is so easy to be swept into the many things that call our attention. The disapproval of fellow adults is much more difficult to ignore and has so many more immediate consequences than the pleas of children for more of our time. When we miss the school's award's ceremony, a softball game, the conference with a teacher — it's easy to justify ourselves. Those of us who both parent and work outside the home walk a tightrope of obligations. The workplace gives at best begrudging recognition to our role as the nurturers of the next generation, so we cheat. We call in sick; we extend the lunch hour; we ask our colleagues to cover, punch us in, brief us on the meeting we skipped. No one ever got a promotion because she made every one of her kid's soccer games.

I try to follow my mother's example of caring for all children by volunteering at our church as a Girl Scout leader. It's more difficult, loving and forgiving children that are not part of your immediate family, although the worst-behaved child at a Scout meeting is usually my own. I find it rewarding to work with girls, supporting their broad interests, enriching their self-esteem, and encouraging their development as whole people. I take them camping to enhance their appreciation of the natural world. We sell Girl Scout cookies to teach the girls that money is real and that they have the ability to earn it. I also participate in Jack and Jill, a social club for African-American mothers and their children. Through Jack and Jill, the children perform regular community service, explore cultural activities, and have their parents' expectations for high achievement reinforced. Participating in this club herself was another way in which my mother met the needs of her own children even as she was an advocate for the needs of all children.

Though my daughter has attended several schools, I commit to volunteering wherever she goes. This country's public schools, especially, need the resources that active parents bring—everything from baking holiday cupcakes to donating computers. Every school can be made better by parents willing to roll up their sleeves and give of their dollars. It's our responsibility to support our own children's schools, and enlightened self-interest should encourage us to support all the schools in our community.

In our accelerated, consumer-driven society, there never seems to be enough time for the life we want to live. I learned from Mother's example that we have priorities, whether established by choice or default. Raising our children must come first; caring for them is not something we can do in our spare time.

Sometimes, when I have a headache and am grumpy from a business trip and my back aches from baking cookies for a school party that my daughter insisted I must provide goodies for, she gives me a big hug with her still-plump arms and says gratefully, "Thanks, Mom." I realize then I need to take a moment to stop and count my blessings. I experience a sense of well-being that only love can provide, and I know how and why my mother put children first.

SERVE

The importance of community service was deeply ingrained in my mother's family. My grandmother felt very deeply the obligation that accompanied the position of privilege that her family occupied relative to the majority of black families in Marion and Perry County, Alabama. She set an example for her children rooted in a statement Jesus made to Peter in the book of Luke, "From everyone to whom much has been given, much will be required." Her children had been given much, through the sacrifices of the early teachers of the Lincoln School.

Marion's Lincoln School owed its existence to the courage

and vision of the town's black leaders working in partnership with the American Missionary Association. Local leaders, including my mother's ancestor James Childs, acquired land for a school, but needed assistance to staff and operate it. After the Civil War, scores of teachers trained in some of the best colleges in New England and the Midwest, converted a religion-inspired abolitionism into a commitment to train leaders among the newly freed slaves. Through the AMA, the teachers were assigned to schools established to educate blacks in the South, where until the war ended, it had been illegal to educate blacks. Theirs was a constant example of extraordinary Christian commitment to service.

One of the legendary teachers of Lincoln was Miss Mary Phillips, a petite, Scots-Irish woman who was the school's principal from 1896 to 1927. My mother's parents were students during her last years, when the school reached its pinnacle. Miss Phillips took a troubled, impoverished school and expanded the campus and student body by the strength of her will and faith. When the school ran out of funds with the boys' dormitory only partly finished, Miss Phillips disappeared for weeks. When she returned, she taught the boys how to make and lay bricks and the students finished the dormitory. Miss Phillips had gone to Tuskegee, still under the leadership of its founder Booker T. Washington, to learn brick work in order to teach it to her students. Ivy was planted along the walls of the dormitory to disguise Miss Phillips' first homemade bricks. This woman was a hero both to the school, which named an auditorium after her, and also to my grandmother, personally. One of Grandmother's last accomplishments was to restore Phillips Hall to public use as a gathering place for graduates of Lincoln and their families. This was the example, the legacy of service that my mother always had before her.

Without the Lincoln School and the sacrifices of its teachers and Miss Phillips, my mother's family would not have had the opportunity to achieve the level and quality of education they possessed. My grandfather's family ran their own businesses, but poverty wages as farm workers or household domestic workers were the usual fate of blacks without education or ownership of their own land. Surrounded by stark examples of the lives led by families who remained trapped by the interplay of poverty and segregation, my grandmother never let her children forget that without the Christian service of others, their lives would be no different. It was the example of these teachers that lifted service to an article of faith in my mother's life.

My grandmother's faith made her a frequent visitor to the homes of those in need: her students, neighbors who were ill, mothers with new babies. She would bring with her some of the bounty of her garden, fresh vegetables or milk for the nursing mother. She would sweep into a home full of good cheer and encouragement, and would seemingly take no notice of the crowded conditions in the small, meanly furnished, unpainted wooden houses. Once I accompanied her to the home of a girl who had just given birth out of wedlock. On the way there, Grandmother expressed deep sorrow over the girl's fate. It broke her heart to see a young person already disadvantaged by poverty fall prey to premature parenthood or alcohol. But she brought presents for the baby and spoke gently to the young mother. I was overwhelmed by the wretchedness of the three-room, bare-walled, wooden structure that was evidently home to a large family. Grandmother, though, behaved with the same kindness and attentiveness as when we visited homes with lace doilies on every surface. She did not look down her nose at anyone. She was too much of a true Christian.

My mother had that same Christian sensibility. She saw the humanity in every person, no matter how poor. My sister Lisa was with Mother one day when they saw a man lying in a slump on the sidewalk. Mother pulled her car over and backed up to where the man was lying. Before Lisa could ask her what she was doing, Mother jumped out of the car and was leaning over the man trying to rouse him from what Lisa assumed was drunkenness. Before Mother could try to lift him into the car, a police officer came over and offered assistance. Mother made the officer promise to get the poor man off the street and to a shelter and he agreed.

At the time Mother became superintendent of the Sunday school at church, there was a growing problem of homelessness in Atlanta that she attributed to the cruel reductions in federal funds for low-income housing. She discovered that ironically, Sunday was a difficult day for homeless people. Many of the shelters served only one meal, children missed the breakfast and lunch that was normally received at school, and public buildings such as libraries were closed. So Mother pushed the congregation to increase their ministry to the homeless. The Atlanta Day Shelter for women was contacted and once a month, members of the congregation drove their Buicks and Volvos to the shelter to pick up mothers and their children to bring them to Sunday school. Once there, the families were given breakfast and invited to participate in classes and Bible Study. For the rest of the day, the church provided sandwiches and activity packs. On Mother's Day, the First Congregational Church had a fifty-year tradition of honoring mothers with a large breakfast of fried chicken, grits, and biscuits. The women from the homeless shelter were included in this hallowed tradition, and so homeless mothers broke bread with mothers who were teachers, lawyers, editors, and businesswomen. It was Christian charity at its finest, in the spirit of the parable on hospitality in the Gospel of Luke: "But when you give a banquet, invite the poor, the crippled, the lame, and the blind. And you will be blessed, because they cannot repay you, for you will be repaid at the resurrection of the righteous."

My mother's most valued friendships were with people who shared her commitment to service. If she joined a club, group, or committee it was usually for the purpose of accomplishing something meaningful. When she was invited to join the social club Jack and Jill, she used it as an opportunity for service. Some of the club's activities were designed to break barriers, to take children to venues that had been previously closed to blacks.

When I was in high school, Mother took charge of one of the Jack and Jill senior-high groups. These groups typically held cotillions, sponsored parties, and spent the year involved in social activities with one service project. Mother turned the entire program upside down, and every activity that entire year was devoted to public service. Mother was a close friend of Father Austin Ford, an Episcopal priest, who ran a settlement house in south Atlanta. There we were each assigned a disadvantaged child to mentor and tutor at least one day a week. We met after school during the week and on Saturdays took the kids on the kind of social outings that Jack and Jill afforded us—roller-skating, bowling, the Six Flags amusement park, swimming. We went all over Atlanta, giving our kids exposure to the world beyond their inner-city neighborhood. As is so often the case with service, it was at least as beneficial to us as to the students we mentored. These children were bright, funny, and engaging, and the time we spent together was quite enjoyable.

This was typical of my mother's approach to social time. Her closest friends were the women with whom she volunteered, such as her sister-in-law Sonjia. The two women became close when they collaborated on a fund-raiser in New York for my father's first Congressional campaign. Sonjia was a former debutante and Ebony Fashion Fair model from Baton Rouge, Louisiana. She was very fashionable and sophisticated. When she married my father's brother, my mother at first didn't quite know what to make of her. Working together on the final arrangements for the New York fund-raiser, they noticed the other women had the names of all their contacts and guests organized on 3-by-5 note cards; Sonjia and Mother had theirs in lists on legal-sized paper. They quickly saw the value of the cards, which could be coded, shuffled, and reorganized with ease. Not to be outdone, Sonjia and Mother spent the evening transferring their lists to 3-by-5 cards. They learned other fund-raising techniques as well, which they continued to use in Atlanta for decades. Mother realized that Sonjia, despite her glamorous exterior, was deeply committed to Christian service. So began a lifelong friendship.

As First Lady of Atlanta, Mother's sense of obligation to serve where she could make a difference increased. Everyone wanted her help with their boards and committees, and she was able to be selective about the projects she took on. "Just let us use your name to attract publicity," committee leaders would plead. But Mother never simply lent her name to a cause or event. The reason the name Jean Young meant so much to begin with was because it had a reputation for being synonymous with enthusiasm and hard work. She generated ideas, made hundreds of phone calls, addressed envelopes, wrote endless personal notes on invitations. My mother worked with Billye Aaron, wife of Hank Aaron, on the Mayor's Masked Ball, an annual fund-raiser for the United Negro College Fund. She cofounded the Atlanta-Fulton County Commission on Children and Youth with Lucy Vance to promote the needs of children in metropolitan Atlanta.

When Mother had a new project, she called together her "Standing Committee of the House"—Sonjia, educator Carolyn McClain, real estate broker Joyce Bacote, mayoral staffer Marian Jones, union activist Alice Johnson, and Sue Ross, a family friend and Atlanta political activist. We called it that because so much of the work on Mother's projects began with these women gathered around her rosewood table in the family room. Recruitment might be intentional or inadvertent, but if you dropped by when Mother was working on a project, you would be given an assignment. Mother would provide food, and there was good fellowship, so working with her was good fun as well as serious business.

I was raised with the conviction that I was to use my education and my abilities to make the world a better place. Growing up, I was surrounded by people who were characterized by their service to others and their communities—Martin Luther King, Jr., and the many folks on the staff of the Southern Christian Leadership Conference; the lawyers for the NAACP Legal Defense Fund, Jack Greenberg and Constance Baker Motley. Even such business leaders as Jesse Hill, President of Atlanta Life Insurance, and Lottie Watkins, founder of a real estate company, I knew more as supporters of voter registration efforts and other community work than as the heads of successful companies.

At an early age, I was sent through our close-knit Atlanta neighborhood with a folder full of little slots to collect funds for the March of Dimes. My sisters and brother and I took UNICEF cans for trick-or-treat on Halloween instead of bags for collecting candy. Mother was always interested in social change and transformation as well as charity, so I was also involved in voter registration long before I was eligible to vote.

My experience with voter registration included an early lesson concerning the requirement of volunteers to abide by the standards and protocols of the organization they serve. As part of an NAACP effort to increase registration in the black community, my mother had agreed to identify neighbors who were not yet registered to vote. I was given a letter to take door-to-door for adults of the residence to read. Each letter had two lines: one allowed the resident to request assistance with voter registration, and the other stated that the person was a registered voter. Each reader could sign his name on the appropriate line. With the arrogance of an eleven-year-old, I thought it silly to stand at the door while people read the letter. So I boldly asked adults whether they were registered to vote. Of course, they all replied that they were registered and needed no information. I returned home, proud of my efficiency.

I couldn't understand why my mother was angry that all the neighbors had affirmed that they were registered voters. She knew better. She explained that the purpose of the letter was to give adults a dignified and discreet way to ask for assistance to become registered voters. When I undermined the confidentiality of the process, I eliminated an element central to the success of the project. It was the first of many lessons I would learn about effective service.

I have endeavored to live up to my mother's legacy of community service through the Girl Scouts and through participation in fund-raising committees and other community projects. I have shelved books in my daughter's school library and planned a major political fund-raiser with First Lady Hillary Clinton as the featured guest. One of my favorite projects was establishing a book fair at our church, Peoples Congregational United Church of Christ. I convened a wonderful committee of talented women and conceived a weekend-long multigenerational event with local authors, music, and a café in the church atrium. The café was extremely popular with our senior citizens, who enjoyed watching the young people swirl about them as they partook in a leisurely chicken dinner. The fellowship hall was transformed into a bookstore with books for every age group, including bestsellers, children's classics, spiritual and African-American titles. Washington-based authors, such as Connie Briscoe, gave readings and autographed their books. Rather than rush away after their readings, most of the authors stayed to hear one another and mingle with the members of the church and community. When I hosted my committee for a thank-you dinner at my home, I was reminded of my mother's "Standing Committee of the House."

I have also tried to follow Mother's example by exposing my daughter to community service early on in her development. Taylor's service activities include: making soup and sandwiches for the homeless; cleaning up public parks, recreational areas, and a Girl Scout campground; and visiting the elderly in nursing homes and performing small errands for them. By fostering the desire to serve her community at a young age, I hope it will become a lifelong practice for her.

When we are looking for meaning in our lives, service is often what is missing. Whether or not you are a religious person, human beings are social and thrive on community. Community service provides a sense of belonging as well as good friendship based on common purpose and values. I find that my most meaningful relationships come through working together on a common project. Among my most trusted friends are women with whom I have planned and organized bookfairs at church and school, Girl Scout camping trips, and fundraisers. I know that a woman who can manage a Girl Scout troop cookie sale will make a dedicated friend.

Today, community service is fashionable. Former chairman of the Joint Chiefs of Staff General Colin Powell is promoting volunteerism; former President George Bush initiated the Points of Light Foundation to encourage volunteers; and increasingly, high school students must earn community-service credits as a requirement for graduation. Americans contribute countless hours of volunteer time.

Typically, community service is designed to ameliorate the conditions of the needy, but we must also look to transform the situation that creates the condition of need. There is a danger that we volunteer to assuage our guilt, then, satisfied that we have done our part, we refuse to make changes or sacrifices to alter the circumstances that made our volunteerism necessary, One can volunteer to read to disadvantaged children, but fail to support funding that would reduce classroom size and allow volunteer tutors to provide enrichment rather than basic support. Hands-on service in a school should lead us to recognize the importance of school reform and to become active champions. My greatest personal challenge is the environment. Every time I drive or use air-conditioning I am conscious of undermining my political efforts to address the crisis of global warming. I am not suggesting that one shouldn't work in a soup kitchen or take dinner to the shut-in elderly unless one is prepared to pay more taxes or raise the minimum wage. Hands-on service can be transformational for both the volunteer and the recipient. And even if one opposes increases in federal food stamp allotments, it is better to feed the poor in soup kitchens than to do nothing at all. But ideally, hands-on community service should open our eyes to the choices we make that perpetuate the very needs we attempt to address with our volunteer work.

The importance of systemic change cannot be overestimated. During the anti-apartheid campaign for a democratic South Africa, the church groups I worked with were concerned over the best way to help the victims of apartheid. We were assured that while the relief funds we raised were appreciated, the most effective action we could take would be to oppose the system through economic sanctions. Archbishop Desmond Tutu traveled around the world giving the message that his people did not want velvet cushions in their apartheid prison. They wanted freedom.

Volunteers engaged in community service are often the most credible advocates for systemic change. Because its volunteers provide direct service to women in shelters, the Junior League is a very persuasive advocate for expanding federal funds to prevent domestic violence. The fight against AIDS, for example, has been so effective due partly to the personal stories many activists can share about the suffering endured by those dying with the disease.

Everyone can serve. Age, education, wealth, even illness are no barriers to community work. When my grandmother was in her seventies, she was busy "helping old people," as she put it. She would escort older church members to their doctor's appointments, take them grocery shopping, and help them prepare meals. The Brownie troop I led planted bulbs around the church in a community beautification project, and older Girl Scouts helped to clean up the Anacostia River. During the anti-apartheid campaign in Washington, I saw cab drivers march in protest alongside Ph.D.'s and get arrested together in front of the South African Embassy. One of the most poignant realities in the movement of international refugees is that during a crisis, the first assistance to refugees is usually given by neighbors nearly as destitute as the refugees themselves. This was true in the Horn of Africa during the Ethiopian crisis and, more recently, with refugees from Kosovo seeking help in Albania. Before the international aid organizations can be mobilized to respond to a crisis, families with barely enough food and water for themselves share both with the refugees. Everyone has something to give.

My grandmother felt a tremendous spiritual calling to return to those less fortunate than herself some measure of the blessings that had been bestowed upon her family. My mother felt this just as intensely, and she had been given so much more than even her mother. Her actions were guided by a desire to follow God's purpose for her life, and she believed that every sacrifice she made was returned to her in bountiful gifts. She gave to the March of Dimes because she had four healthy children free of any disabling conditions. She cared for the homeless because she had never lacked food and shelter.

Even after Mother was diagnosed with cancer, she did not withdraw from her community involvements. She continued to do as much as her health and strength would allow. She had had an operation to remove a cancerous growth and was on a regimen of chemotherapy when the Governor of Georgia proposed reductions in the funds available through the federal program for aid to families with dependent children. Children's activists planned a press conference and rally to protest the proposed cuts. My mother brought fabric paint and rolls of yellow and green light plastic sheeting to cut and design signs. She knew the small children could not carry big signs or wear heavy sandwich boards, so she created a kind of soft, two-sided bib with slogans on the front and back.

The night before the rally, my mother and I and several of her Committee members sat around the rosewood table in the family room, making bibs and using the paint to write the slogan: "Don't balance the budget on our backs." Early the next morning, my mother had a chemotherapy treatment. Afterward, she sat in her car and watched the rally from across the street while I delivered her remarks at the rally. It was so symbolic of the generous and giving way she lived her life—to serve, not for recognition or acclaim, but out of personal conviction, faith in God, and a desire to share a portion of the many gifts with which her life had been blessed.

EVERY CHILD
CAN LEARN

Throughout her adult life, my mother was an educator. Her work was characterized by creativity and innovation: she believed that every child can learn, and that it is the responsibility of adults to provide the appropriate setting and resources to nurture the abilities of each child.

My mother never taught in the "best" schools, in affluent private or suburban schools. Rather, she taught in an inner-city school in Hartford, Connecticut, where the children were given showers twice a week to ensure proper hygiene that they may not have received at home. She taught in a segregated school in south Georgia, where harvest and planting took precedence over education for many of the older students. She taught in the schools of Atlanta, where her students were grateful to live in public housing. Despite or perhaps because she worked with the least-privileged students, she believed in their possibilities.

Her first job in Atlanta was teaching at Whitefoord Elementary School. Although several years had passed since the Supreme Court decision in *Brown v. Board of Education,* Atlanta maintained a segregated school system. As the composition of the Whitefoord's neighborhood had changed from poor white to poor black, the all-white school had been closed and the school reopened for a black student body with a new principal and faculty. The students were drawn from Capitol Homes, a public housing complex composed of garden apartments within view of the gold-leafed dome of the Georgia State Capitol. As a teacher new to the school system, Mother felt a great deal of pressure to prove herself. The principal at Whitefoord had handpicked his faculty from among the strongest young black teachers available. Most of the Whitefoord teachers went on to become principals themselves.

In one of the early faculty meetings in which the students were divided up among grade levels, a number of struggling students moving into second grade were discussed. The usual practice was to divide these difficult students evenly among the second-grade teachers, but Mother asked to take them all. The other teachers protested that some of these children had not yet learned to read. Mother assured her colleagues that when the students left her class, every child would be reading. She staked her reputation on her belief in the ability of these children to learn.

During the course of the school year, Mother supplemented the school curriculum with her own materials. She brought in literature for the children to use in their reading groups and created mimeographed phonics lessons. Both techniques were innovations in the Atlanta system in 1962, when old-fashioned Dick-and-Jane-style readers were still used. Whitefoord's principal was skeptical of these deviations. But with diplomacy and patience, she explained the reasoning behind her use of phonics and what she had learned from her studies at Queens College in New York. Her quiet persistence was persuasive, and her use of these unsanctioned approaches was not forbidden. When the year ended, Mother had kept her promise. All the children in her second-grade class were able to read and were prepared for third grade.

A few years later, Atlanta implemented a desegregation order by restructuring each school faculty to reflect the proportion of black and white teachers in the school system as a whole. Mother was transferred to Slaton Elementary School located in Cabbagetown, a neighborhood of company-built houses in the shadow of the city's old cotton mills. The mills were closed, but Cabbagetown remained an enclave of the white working poor. Mother's work plan with the students included home visits, which she approached with some degree of trepidation. She wondered how Southern white parents would accept a black teacher. My mother was pleasantly surprised to find that the respect for her status as teacher took precedence over the customs of segregation. What mattered to the parents was not her color, but her concern for the educational attainment of their children. She never forgot how committed even the most disadvantaged parents could be to give their own children a chance to learn and achieve.

Schools in Atlanta varied by class as well as race. Although black schools had the worst buildings and the oldest classroom materials, the schools in poor white neighborhoods were also inferior to the schools in middle-class white neighborhoods. Mother's commitment and achievements in raising the educational level of her students impressed the principal at Slaton. Having demonstrated that she could work effectively with black and white students, and having established a glowing record as an innovator, Mother was recommended for a position that allowed her to train new teachers.

The Teacher Corps program, an anti-poverty initiative of President Lyndon Johnson, was based on the notion that to break the cycle of poverty, the teachers of low-income children should be particularly well trained. My mother served as a "lead teacher," mentoring and supervising new teachers as they applied innovative techniques to challenge students. She impressed upon her student teachers the importance of believing in their students' potential, sharing her own experience in the classroom.

Mother's student teachers were given the same caring attention she expected them to show their own pupils, modeling what she taught. One of the students was a young woman from the Philippines. Knowing that Sonya was a long way from her family, Mother brought her home to dinner, helped her adapt American ingredients to prepare meals familiar to her palate, and generally smoothed her transition to the United States.

My sister Paula followed my mother into a career in education and relied on her advice and counsel. Her first teaching position was in a school that drew students from Carver Homes, a large public housing development. She was so steeped in my mother's educational philosophy that she was shocked at the low expectations for her students—some of whom were the third generation in their families on public assistance. The students came to school with very limited preparation, but Paula understood that it was their environment rather than a lack of innate intelligence that accounted for their limited vocabulary. One student thought that the word for cup was "coffee." Paula searched for cues on how to reach her kindergarten students and discovered that many of them had a talent for memorization. She had them memorize stories, then memorize the written words to the story. This built their confidence and increased the number of words the children could read by sight.

Paula asked her school's music teacher to help her teach the children "Lift Every Voice and Sing," the Negro national anthem and an important part of the heritage of these African-American students. The music teacher refused, because she didn't believe the children could learn a song with such a challenging vocabulary. Using a tape recorder, Paula taught the class the song herself along with hand and arm movements. At the closing assembly of the school year, Paula's students performed "Lift Every Voice and Sing" in front of the entire school. Nearly all of her students passed to first grade as competent readers.

One of my mother's favorite illustrations about the power teachers have to affect their students involved an experiment where children were selected at random and assigned to a teacher who was told that these were gifted children and had scored exceptionally high on aptitude tests. At the end of the school year, these children had made exceptional progress in their studies. The teacher's belief that they were all gifted seemed to influence their level of performance, and they achieved at levels that would have been expected for a class of specially selected gifted students. In fact, these were ordinary students and their high achievement was a real surprise.

As a new teacher, Paula was sent to observe a model

classroom where she saw the other side of the expectations effect. The teacher had the children divided into working groups. From the door of the classroom, it was immediately apparent to Paula which group was considered the best by the encouraging inflection of the teacher's voice and the array of materials they had to work with. The children were coloring work sheets, and while the children in the highest group had an array of crayons, the children in the low group had only one crayon each. To Paula, this was a classic case of low expectations crushing children's chance to learn. She could not imagine the justification for denying children even the choice of colors they use in a worksheet. She knew the message to the children was that they were too stupid to be trusted with more than one crayon.

Mother was able to harness the positive expectations of an entire city to encourage student achievement with her unique career fair—the Dream Jamboree. While a candidate for Mayor of Atlanta, my father pledged to find ways to use his office to promote public education. Once he was elected, my mother established the Mayor's Task Force on Education, which she chaired. She perceived that as Mayor, my father brought to the city a number of unique resources, not the least of which were his contacts with colleges around the nation. She would bring representatives of those colleges to Atlanta to meet high school students, thus expanding the college opportunities for students in Atlanta. The city would provide all the networking and information that college-educated parents were able to provide for their youngsters. Mother conceived a career fair to inspire high school students to prepare for "a life worth dreaming about." Her focus was expanding the possibilities for students who were not already college-bound, for those who believed that college was out of their reach.

My mother approached the Atlanta school superintendent with the Dream Jamboree concept and two critical principles. The first was that every student in an eligible grade would attend; this would not be a reward for the best students, but an opportunity to widen the horizons of the poorest students. The second principle was that the Jamboree would be for both the younger and the older students. Ninth and tenth graders would attend, as well as the about-to-graduate eleventh and twelfth graders. Mother met with great opposition to the novel idea that ninth graders would respond to an opportunity to plan their high school courses in conjunction with career goals. But with her customary persistence, Mother convinced the superintendent and other officials that by eleventh grade, many students had missed the opportunity to prepare for the career they wanted—failing to take the requisite math and science courses. Her view prevailed.

My mother and her committee recruited exhibitors for the career fair from a wide variety of career options—apprenticeship and skills training programs; technical schools; military branches and institutions; corporations; the government;

as well as colleges and universities. She invited recruiters from every college that had awarded my father an honorary degree or where he had given a speech. As a result, private schools with scholarship money and schools as far away as Colby College in Maine and Lincoln University of Missouri, put Atlanta's Dream Jamboree on their recruitment travel schedule. Mother approached Jim Davis, an executive at the Georgia Power Company, and requested an in-kind donation—the printing of the Dream Jamboree Career Planning Handbook. Each eligible student received the handbook with more than 120 pages of basic information about every exhibitor, a career planning guide, academic requirements for graduation, and instructions for wisely using the time at the Dream Jamboree. In addition to exhibitors' booths, the Jamboree hall featured multimedia presentations to highlight career options that students may not have considered.

The three days of the Dream Jamboree were organized with almost military precision to ensure that every one of the 15,000 students would have an opportunity to reach out to at least three exhibitors. The students were instructed to select in advance the booths they wanted to visit. During the Jamboree, Mother would walk the floor of the exhibit hall, encouraging students and recruiters. She prodded the recruiters to be more aggressive, urging them to reach out to the students. "Don't wait for them to come over to the booth," she would say. Mother was concerned for the shy student, the student who would be intimidated, the student who was insecure. If she saw a student looking bewildered, she would take his hand, lead him to a booth, and help him start a conversation with a recruiter.

The Dream Jamboree exposed students to many schools whose admission criteria were within reach of average students, and to those that would take a chance on students without sterling academic credentials. One small college in North Carolina, Warren Wilson, came to the Dream Jamboree, although it had no tradition of recruiting in Atlanta. That college combines academic classes with hands-on work opportunities. Its students handle computer work for administrative offices, work in local cattle and forestry operations, and even help build school facilities. As a result of the Dream Jamboree, several Atlanta students receive work-study scholarships to Warren Wilson each year.

An outgrowth of the Dream Jamboree was the mayor's Scholars Program. The Equitable, a financial services company and Jamboree supporter, offered to fund a scholarship as well. The Mayor's Task Force on Education, which Mother chaired, developed an essay contest to select one student from each region of the school district and one at-large student. The winners would receive a $1,000 college scholarship. My mother wanted the students' essays to be judged on creativity rather than academic merit. She wanted to use the scholarship to identify bright students who didn't necessarily excel in high school in traditional ways. One of the first students to become a Mayor's scholar went on to be the valedictorian at Syracuse University.

Along with Jamboree's practical advice and conversations with recruiters came an important message—*We believe in you.* The Jamboree is a compact with Atlanta school kids; if they have a good academic record, the Dream Jamboree will help them match their aspirations with a college or career program. When my father left the Mayor's office, the college scholarships awarded to Atlanta high school students had increased from $6 million to more than $20 million. Subsequent mayors and school superintendents have maintained a commitment to the Dream Jamboree, making it an Atlanta institution.

Believing deeply that creativity is much needed to elicit the best from every child, my mother explored a number of ways to inject innovation into education. She worked with the IBM corporation to develop a multimedia lesson on American history and culture using focal points like Martin Luther King's "Letter from the Birmingham Jail." She worked with a company that developed a video encyclopedia, a precursor to the CDs that now come packaged with every new desktop computer.

Mother was an early advocate of the Writing to Read program, in which at-risk four-year-olds can develop a level of proficiency with standard English, vocabulary, and computers. More than a decade ago, she encouraged its introduction into the Gate City Day Nursery system of child-care centers for low-income children. Writing to Read is now widely used in schools in the U.S. and abroad. Mother was a founding board member of SciTrek, a hands-on science museum, and the APEX, an African-American History museum. These institutions and programs share the philosophy that kids can learn, given the right stimulation and inspiration. Mother understood that diversity of experience was essential. Not every child will respond to the same stimuli.

Quality education is virtually an obsession with American parents, especially college-educated parents. It is a subject about which no one with children can afford to be complacent. While there is a lot of talk and debate about schools and education, our country's way of funding schools through local property taxes leaves the poorest, least-advantaged kids with the poorest, least-equipped schools. Older, poorer communities have a great deal more difficulty financing quality schools, even as their school populations need more special education and other programs. In the public schools of Washington, D.C., the buildings have physically deteriorated and there is no system in place for renovation. This state of affairs is contrary to everything my mother believed in. A school system and school board should start with the premise that every child can learn, and then work backwards to determine how best to nurture a love of learning in every child. Instead, the approach seems to be—this is how we will teach, and it's up to the child to learn it.

Despite the state of the Washington, D.C., school system, several years ago I started my daughter in the public school in my middle-class neighborhood. I believe in the importance of public education, and feel that parents should support the schools to enable them to be more effective. In my daughter's school I found some wonderful teachers, some innovative programs, and a number of committed, dedicated parents. In the end, it wasn't the school itself but decisions made at the top that led me to withdraw Taylor from public school.

My daughter's last year in public school began one recent summer when fire-code violations in scores of schools meant that they had to be repaired under court order before the schools could open. As the first day of school approached in September, many code violations went unresolved. When I told my child that the opening of school would be delayed, she burst into tears. I was faced with a decision—to demonstrate that this result was unacceptable or to acquiesce. I chose to begin an immediate search for a new school. A psychologist who administered the requisite, initial battery of placement tests confirmed that my daughter had not been in an educational environment that met her needs and challenged her abilities.

I wanted so much to discuss with my mother my decision

to change schools, since she was such an advocate for public schools. But, first and foremost she was an advocate for children. Her values would place the needs of the child first. That year my daughter was enrolled in an independent school for girls.

The refreshing difference we now experience at the Holton-Arms School is the constant innovation to meet the educational needs of the girls. The school is never static. Teachers introduce new programs like design technology. They integrate computer skills as a research tool, and they've recently added wind and percussion instruments to the music program. There is a responsiveness to the needs of the students that was lacking in Taylor's former school. That responsiveness and innovation should be a core feature of our public school system. The mandate to educate every child requires more, not less innovation, and diversity of educational strategies.

My daughter has a wonderfully creative imagination for writing, but her mind races faster than she can manually write. As early as fourth grade, her teachers allowed her to type many of her writing assignments. Her school offers keyboarding classes for students of all ages before and after school. Taylor may never develop beautiful penmanship, but she no longer complains about writing assignments. I'll admit that chatting online via e-mail and instant messaging has improved her typing speed even more.

Taylor's fifth-grade teacher advised her father and me to review math with her during the summer, since Holton-Arms students begin to receive grades in math in sixth grade. Math is not Taylor's strongest subject, and it was not an area where I could really help her. A member of my church, Dr. Brenda Hammond, had just received a Presidential Award for her excellence in teaching math. She agreed to work with Taylor and a friend for a few sessions. Taylor was not too eager to spend part of her summer vacation in this way, but she reluctantly agreed to give it a try. Dr. Hammond directed the girls in a manner that reinforced what they knew and built their confidence. Rather than criticize wrong answers, she asked them to explain their answers and their methods. At the end of the first hour, my daughter was begging for more time to spend on math. Instead of worrying about math class, my daughter will enter sixth grade feeling confident in her ability.

As good a student as my daughter is, flexible and innovative interventions have helped her work to her potential. For a student on the brink of failure, the absence of creative and affirming teachers may push him out of the schoolhouse door. The challenge for parents is to be advocates for their children. If a child's current school is not responsive, find another or supplement what the school is doing with other learning activities. This summer my daughter attended a week-long day camp at the SciTrek Museum in Atlanta. The sessions are geared to specific age levels and are designed to make science fun. In Taylor's group, the children used science to solve mysteries. I was particularly pleased that the instructor was a young woman, a recent graduate of Spelman College. Programs at colleges, museums, zoos, and other institutions can provide educational opportunities for a child to supplement the learning she receives in school.

As a testament to my mother's commitment to children and learning, the parents' association at Southwest middle school, near my parent's home in southwest Atlanta, moved rapidly after her death to rename the school for her. Originally a high school, Southwest is where my sister Lisa and I received our high school diplomas. Paula began her high school career at Southwest, but went on to finish at the United Nations International School in New York. A new high school was built and Southwest became the neighborhood's middle school. The year my mother died, it was renovated with a state-of-the-art multimedia center, upgraded science labs, and a dynamic new principal. On the first day of school, there was a dedication ceremony attended by the superintendent and a number of local dignitaries. My father gave the school a formal portrait of Mother to hang in the entry and some mementos so that her image and her values would be real to the students and faculty.

Touring the building after the ceremony, I saw a young teacher introduce himself to his students with an airplane crossing the room on a line above their heads. He told them they would spend the year learning about what they had just seen and building models to explore different scientific theories. My mother would have been pleased to see this exciting new teacher. The Jean Childs Young Middle School stands as a constant reminder of my mother's belief that every child can learn, and of the community's responsibility to ensure that every child has the chance to do so.

A KISS WILL
MAKE IT BETTER

Mother had a special gift for nurturing all who came within her circle. She was the center of our immediate family and a larger extended family of relatives, close personal friends, and friends in the struggle for justice. She knew that she could comfort and soothe with her presence, and she believed it was her responsibility to try.

A sought-after speaker for Women's Day at churches in Atlanta, my mother used her speeches to encourage women to work for equal pay and equal rights. She often went through a roll call of women achievers, including Eleanor Roosevelt and Mary McLeod Bethune. She incorporated the woman-affirming poetry of Maya Angelou. But she also celebrated the role women played as nurturers. In one speech, she wrote:

> *We as women have so much to offer*
> *But our giving begins with our families*
> *The center where God resides*
> *If we fail here*
> *How can we move into the world?*
> *Women have a special responsibility*
> *When our children talk to us—listen*
> *When our husbands need encouragement—offer a warm embrace*
> *When our sisters and brothers need a kind word—offer it*
> *When our parents need love and patience—provide it*

Confronted with an injured child, my mother's response was to comfort. No matter how minor the injury—a splinter or a scratch—if it was painful to the child, she took it seriously. I remember how she comforted my brother, who at age two was seventeen years younger than me. After scraping his knee while playing in the steep driveway in front of our house, he ran toward the house crying for his mother. She rushed outside and scooped him up into her arms. She sat down with him in her lap to find the wound, and she kissed the hurt knee to take the pain away. Then she spanked the offending pavement which inflicted the injury. "Bad driveway," she said, hugging Bo close with her other arm. My little brother quickly learned to spank the offending objects himself, but only once he was safely encircled in our mother's arms. When Mother saw me looking on, she explained to me that children are so entirely self-centered that they may blame themselves for their own accidents. She spanked the offending object (instead of the child) to dramatize to the child that she or he was not at fault.

My sister Paula has a vivid recollection of keeping an eye on our brother Bo in the sixth-floor apartment my parents maintained in Washington, D.C. The furnishings were very modern and included a glass-topped coffee table. While Mother prepared dinner, Paula concentrated on ensuring that Bo did not sneak onto the balcony unattended. Bo began to amuse himself by jumping up and down on the sofa, and then suddenly he was crashing headfirst into the table, crying and bleeding. Mother rushed in and took him into the bathroom to clean his face and identify the source of the blood. As it turned out, a baby tooth had been loosened by the fall and it was only his mouth that was bleeding. Paula was crying with fear and shame. How could she have let her baby brother fall that way? With Bo in one arm, Mother sat down next to Paula and put her other arm around her and gave her a hug. Secure in her mother's love, Paula stopped crying.

The magic and importance of Mother's hugs and kisses were that they spared you from internalizing the pain. All too often we respond to our honest mistakes with shame and allow them to become a judgment on our self-worth. For my sisters and brother and I, our mother's intervention prompted an externalization of the pain, and directed the blame away from the child in pain. With the pain banished, the child could then be exhorted to try again—to climb the monkey bars, to ride the bicycle, to build the tower.

By the time I was six, I was so convinced of my mother's power to make it better that I didn't cry when injured. I remember a day I walked home from school. It had just rained, and I began to take a shortcut up the front lawn rather than use the steps. Then I slipped, hitting my head on the retaining wall by the driveway. I calmly and silently got to my feet and walked inside to show my mother, who hugged me, kissed my forehead, and cleaned the wound. I still have the scar and the memory of the sense of well-being that her presence could bring.

My father spent endless days and nights organizing marches in hostile cities, recruiting and training civil rights activists in nonviolent social action, and negotiating with opponents of civil rights. He wrote letters home almost daily, confiding his fears and frustrations to my mother. He ended his letters with a prayer to be with her again and to thereby be refreshed and renewed.

Until I read one of those letters, I couldn't understand some of my father's travel decisions. When he had the opportunity to come home, he did. If he had to be in Washington for a meeting on Thursday, say, and in Chicago on Saturday, he would go home to Atlanta on Friday, a one-thousand-mile detour. Luckily, Atlanta is an easy airport to fly in and out of, but I don't think it would have mattered. My mother's caring and attention was as vital to my father as food and water.

My father's mother was a strong-willed, self-sufficient woman, but even she came to rely on my mother's care. While she loved my mother's parents, she had hoped her eldest son would have married a local New Orleans girl. She lived in the two-story brick home she and my grandfather built in the 1940s until she was eighty-four, when she suffered a bad fall. Without hesitation, my mother brought Gram into her home and tried to make her as comfortable as possible. The furniture from Gram's bedroom was brought to Atlanta and set up to resemble as closely as possible her room in New Orleans. Gram was a fabulous Creole cook, and Mother deferred to her in the kitchen. My grandmother was an avid bridge player, and Mother located a group of senior citizens who played bridge regularly. Gram was not much for praise and I don't think she ever complimented my mother directly. But one night, when my husband and Gram were drinking a Coke in the kitchen, she confided with a sigh, "You know, Tony, Jean has always been good to me."

My mother refused to believe that there was a contradiction in a woman's dual role as nurturer and as professional. Neither did she believe that only women could nurture. She bragged about her two older brothers, Bill and Norman, and their support and protectiveness to her as they all grew up. Norman, who eventually made his career designing uniforms for the military, created clothes for his sister's dolls. Bill was his mother's right arm and surrogate when she and his father were at work. Bill would prepare meals for the younger children, clean house, and bandage scrapes. The summer of a polio epidemic, during which parents were urged to keep their children isolated, Bill built a playground with a seesaw and whirlygig for his two young sisters, using scraps of wood and metal. My mother adored her oldest brother. When he married and moved to Tuskeegee, she enjoyed visiting and helping Bill and his wife, Barbara, with their babies.

As a teenager and a young adult, I developed a reputation for independence and self-sufficiency. I traveled to Europe with a study tour at thirteen, went out of state to college at seventeen, and spent the summer after my freshman year conducting door-to-door surveys in New England for a Children's Defense Fund report, *Children Out of School.* I attribute my autonomy to my mother's teaching and the reassurance that if I couldn't handle my disappointments, I could turn to her for relief and comfort.

At the age of three, my brother, Bo, was protected by his secure relationship with our mother. He was in my uncle's pool, holding on to the edge, while my mother and aunt sat by the side chatting and watching. Bo slipped off into the water, which was over his head. It took a moment for my mother to notice that his head was no longer visible. Immediately, she waded to the spot where she had last seen her son and lifted him from the water. Bo took a deep breath. When he lost his hold on the side, he had held his breath as he had been taught, and waited for his mother to rescue him. His utter confidence that she would do so probably prevented a tragedy.

When my youngest sister, Paula, was in elementary school, it was still against the rules for girls to wear pants. Our father had traveled to India, and among the gifts he brought back were brightly colored long silk tunics with baggy pants to be worn underneath. Paula wanted desperately to wear hers, but she knew that pants were prohibited. Then Mother gave her the security to wear the outfit; she told her they were not pants, they were called *shalwar-qamiz*. Sure enough, when Paula arrived at school, she was sent to the office for violating the rules. Paula bravely informed the principal that she was not wearing pants, she was wearing shalwar-qamiz, a national dress worn by women in India. Rather than being sent home, Paula spent the rest of the day going from class to class showing other students her outfit and sharing stories about India. She could take the risk of confronting school rules because she knew that Mother was behind her.

My first children were the son and daughter of my husband's previous marriage. In our early years together, I endeavored to provide for them the kind of nurturing home environment in which I had grown up. As we tried to merge family styles, I found that family and holiday meals were tension-filled. When the children came to visit, I would take pains to prepare a room, making the beds with fresh sheets and setting out matching towels. I would buy groceries so their father could prepare their favorite meals, and encourage them to invite friends to dinner. I hosted holiday dinners that included their mother, my husband's ex-wife. But there was no correlation between the effort I put into caring for them and the sense of well-being they seemed to receive from it. I felt my best efforts were met with wariness, and even resentment.

My mother was the center of her family and home. With that as my model, I was completely unprepared for rejection as I attempted to step into a role ministering to the needs of the family and healing their physical and psychic hurts. In my family, I began to feel I was a source of pain rather than a source of comfort. I had begun with great hopes that I could gather my husband and stepchildren into one big happy family, but I did not succeed. On the other hand, my stepchildren loved my mother.

I tried, almost desperately, to adopt my mother's style in a blended family. So much so that I worried whether the flaw was in me. Finally, my own daughter was born and it was a blessing to have someone whose needs I could fill. I could feed her and she'd stop crying. I could kiss and cuddle her and she would sigh with contentment. With her, I had the ability to give comfort that my mother seemed to have with so many people.

As was not the case with my stepchildren, Taylor and I were together from the beginning and I was able to use the things my mother had taught by example. When Taylor got her finger squeezed in the kitchen door, I kissed it and made her feel better. When she began to walk and bumped her head on the dining room table, I kissed it and spanked the table. It was a joy to me for her to bring me her bruises and scratches, to come to me for solace.

As Taylor grows, it is social situations, things that people say or do that hurt her. She brings them to me and we talk them through. Girls tend to be very sophisticated about social relationships, but Taylor is straightforward and sometimes naive. Once I met her after a bus trip and she was crying because an older girl had been taunting her in a manner that everyone on the bus could hear. I held her until she calmed down. As she told the story, I helped Taylor to see that the shame belonged to the other girl for behaving so badly. There might be ways that Taylor could have diffused the situation and handled it differently, but she should not accept responsibility for someone else's poor behavior.

Taylor has now achieved such a measure of self-sufficiency that she was willing to spend two weeks at overnight camp without a friend to accompany her. As we waited for the camp gates to open, she jumped out of the car and began strolling up the line of cars to look for girls her age and campers from the previous year. In her exploration, she found two friends, one old and one new. When her father and I were given her cabin assignment, she grabbed a top bunk, pushed her trunk beneath the bottom bed, and told us goodbye. She wrote one letter expressing her homesickness, and later wrote that while she missed us, she could manage it. She knew I would come for her if the feelings of sadness and loneliness overwhelmed the adventure of camp.

Our world is so complex, and the pace of change increases relentlessly. Our families need an anchor, a center, a source of sustaining love and nurturing. Mothers and fathers can be that anchor for their children, and couples can be that anchor for each other. A close friend may provide the comfort and support that we need. Although my mother believed nurturing was a special calling for women, it is not the exclusive province of women.

Through word and deed Mother taught me, and I am teaching my daughter that, secure in the knowledge that we are loved, we can meet the challenges of life. There may be pain, but we can persevere as long as we know there is a safe harbor for renewal, a loved one to provide a soothing embrace.

BE A HOMEMAKER,
NOT A HOUSEWIFE

An important part of my mother's life's work was making a home—a home for her husband and children, a home that welcomed friends old and new. But there was no description of a woman's role that annoyed my mother more than the term "housewife." "I am not married to my house," she would say. Homemaking, to her, was all about hospitality and comfort. *Housewifery* was about cleaning and order. While Mother liked cleanliness and order, it was not high on her list of personal priorities. She was too busy creating a place of warmth and and comfort for her family.

    MAD magazine was a favorite when I was a kid. I have

never forgotten one of its pieces in which a child is admonished to stay out of the living room, *"You know the living room is for nobody."* As American homes have grown, we seem to have more and more rooms for nobody. My husband likes to joke that the front parlor used to be for the minister, now no one sits there but door-to-door sales people. Even the minister is escorted downstairs to the "rec room." Our formal rooms are symbols that we have arrived in the middle class, but they also intimidate us. At parties, guests often tend to cluster in the kitchen for psychic safety.

I once attended a fund-raiser for my daughter's school where the guests paid more than $100 per person for a buffet supper. Everyone was dressed in what we used to refer to as "after five" attire. The hosts were happy to show off their newly remodeled and beautifully decorated home. But even these well-dressed folks gravitated to the warmth of the family room. The elegant formal living room was virtually empty.

This syndrome occurs in the most modest homes. My family's old neighborhood in Atlanta was comprised of small brick homes with a living room, dining room, kitchen, and three bedrooms. It was not uncommon for the living room and dining room to be maintained in spotless condition and always unoccupied. Families took meals in the kitchen crowded around a table that might comfortably seat two adults and two children.

In my mother's home, all the rooms were for everybody. She decorated to invite, to welcome, and to make her guests and family members comfortable. My father loved to fall asleep on the couch reading or watching a football game on Sunday afternoon. So she furnished the house with long, well-padded couches that were comfortable to sleep on and easy to clean. The dining room table had leaves, so that it could be expanded to accommodate everyone who showed up for dinner. She liked open spaces in rooms, to maintain flexibility and to leave floorspace for small children to play. Decorating was personal expression for Mother, and her way of providing a home that suited the needs of its inhabitants.

Mother decorated the children's rooms and allowed each one to express the individual personality of its occupant. This was very progressive on her part, to allow us children free rein in that way. My youngest sister wanted a room decorated in hot pink, purple, and green Mardi Gras colors. My mother tracked down wallpaper and matching bedclothes that included all of those hues. She covered one wall with cork so that my sister could post all of her posters of the latest musical heartthrobs, her certificates for swimming, award ribbons, and anything else that she wanted to express herself.

After spending three years in New York while my father was U.S. Ambassador to the United Nations, my mother finally had the time and money to redecorate her entire home. The Atlanta house had been rented while they were away, and it needed a top-to-bottom refreshing with new carpet and walls repainted in every room. Mother relished this project, and set a color scheme for each room. She took great care with my brother's room, giving him a red, white, and blue decor and plenty of storage for his treasures. Always, form and design were secondary to function.

When I bought my first home, an old-fashioned white frame house in the West End section of Atlanta, my mother gave me one fully decorated room as a housewarming gift. She and my Aunt Sonjia measured a grungy back room and turned it into a lovely sitting chamber with coordinated mauve floor and wall coverings.

Decorating allowed my mother to release her artistic instincts. It was also part of the example set by her own mother. Idella Childs had expressed her artistry through her dressmaking and through the quilts and upholstery she crafted. Her bedrooms each had color themes, with the drapes, throw pillows and bedspreads made from the same fabric or coordinating fabrics. Her bedroom was blue, the guest room green and yellow, the spare bedroom pink and white. Miss Idella upholstered her antique sofa, love seat, and matching chairs with heavy brocade, then made tufted pillows to match.

Despite the sofa's complicated upholstery done in costly fabrics, Grandmother never scolded us grandchildren for sitting on it. If she found us playing with the china bric-a-brac on the marble-topped coffee table, she would tell the story of where the piece came from, and which of her children brought it back from his or her travels. The minister and other guests were received in the living room. Like my mother's home, my grandmother's house was full of the clutter of life and living. Her mantle was crammed with photos of wedding, graduations, and family portraits of her five children, fourteen grandchildren, and eventually, her great-grandchildren. She had albums full of clippings from my cousins, the football players. She kept yearbooks and graduation programs and mementos of every kind.

My grandmother's sitting room was even more congested. At one end was her sewing machine. When I was a child, it seemed my grandmother only sat down while she was at her sewing machine and in church. At all other times she was in motion, and even at her sewing machine her hands were constantly moving, pinning, snipping, and sliding fabric under the pumping needle. The sitting room contained file drawers stuffed with materials for her Girl Scout troop, her historic preservation efforts, her political activities, her Lincolnite Alumni Association, and records from the First Congregational Church. At the other end of the room were stacks of albums containing family photographs dating back to the nineteenth century. Grandmother never apologized for the clutter; I don't think she even noticed it. The clutter represented her memories of yesterday and all the things she intended to accomplish tomorrow. Her life was about helping people and making a difference. Her front door was always metaphorically open and if she knew you were coming over, she would tidy up.

My mother grew up in a different house from the one I knew as my grandparent's home. It was a lovely gingerbread-trimmed farmhouse that was eventually destroyed because of road construction. In that house, the center of activity was the dining room. It was there the children did their homework, Miss Idella sewed, and everyone listened to the radio. With so much activity, the room was seldom orderly. When company came, it could be straightened up in lightning speed.

I always appreciated my good fortune in having a mother who was not obsessed with cleaning the house. On beautiful Saturday mornings, I was out playing when other girls in my neighborhood were still doing chores. Our housework was directed at maintaining basic hygiene rather than cleaning a floor so we'd be able to eat off of it. Mother focused on fresh, clean sheets, rather than a perfectly made bed. She refused to expend all of her energy on keeping an immaculate house. It was neither her priority nor her inclination. She thought it acceptable for a home to look lived in, rather than like a hotel with no permanent residents.

Unlike so many black women of their generations, neither my mother nor her mother had ever been in service as domestic workers. Some of the compulsion that I saw growing up about maintaining a spotless home was because women who worked cleaning for others wanted the same standard upheld in their own homes. While that was understandable, it was possibly only through extraordinary effort and self-discipline. Writer Alice Walker justly celebrated such women as "head-ragged generals" who paved the way for their daughters to obtain an education and earn a living with books instead of mops.

When I was a teenager, I moved into a room in the basement level of our house that had once been marketed as a mother-in-law suite. I had a private bathroom and two large closets. My room was painted electric yellow, and Mother helped me wallpaper the ceiling with all my favorite psychedelic posters. My room was out of sight and out of mind. Since it was a danger to no one but me, Mother didn't argue about its lack of order. She remarked thoughtfully that some of her friends with daughters my age spent a lot of time arguing about cleaning their rooms. She thought the relationship between a teenaged daughter and her mother was too fragile to jeopardize over issues like that.

When I had my own home, I never had to worry that a visit from my mother meant a white-glove inspection. A freshly made bed, clean towels, and a light pickup of clutter were all she expected. She came to see us—her grandchild, really—not the house. Still, I once found her cleaning my refrigerator. She didn't fuss at me, but was almost apologetic. "It's easier to do this in someone else's house, you know." She took great care to let me know that she was being helpful; she wasn't implying a criticism of my housekeeping skills.

As much as I love a clean house and admire those who

have one, cleaning is at the bottom of my list of priorities. The people within the house get priority over the house itself. There are only so many hours in the day. When my daughter was young, we would come in the house after work and day care and make dinner. The dinner dishes and cleanup would then simply have to wait while I gave Taylor her bath, set out her clothes for the next day, and shared quiet time talking and reading aloud. Only when she was finally asleep did I get to the dishes. If I ran downstairs to load the dishwasher while she was in the tub, I might have failed to hear her call for help if there was soap in her eyes or a toy she wanted. After being away from her the entire day, I felt that for a couple of hours she was entitled to my full attention.

Now that she's older, Taylor can help with getting dinner on the table and some chores. But she's still a child who needs attention. Our tradition of quiet evening now encompasses our each silently reading our own books, then my reading aloud to her. Sometimes she wants to play a game of backgammon or mancala. These are opportunities for me to hear what is on her mind, how things went for her during the day, her hopes and her anxieties.

Mothers have at least two or three full-time jobs, depending on paid employment and the extent of their community service activity. Something has to give. I see women with children working from dawn until midnight organizing the home, preparing meals, shuttling children around, supervising homework and extracurricular activities. Add to that eight to ten hours a day at a paying job and there is simply not enough time to do justice to all of these roles. To that mix many of us include church and other volunteer work. It's no wonder that classes and books on organization are so popular.

If I ask myself what matters most—a clean kitchen or snuggle time with my daughter—the answer is very clear. An impulse to clean the kitchen has much to do with what other people think, and listening to one's inner voice is what's hard about making choices and setting your own priorities. You can use your time to impress the neighbors or you can use it to do the things that you believe bring real value to your life.

My house includes all of the elements: china, silver chafing dishes, platters to entertain with formal sit-down dinners. I use all my best tableware for special family dinners—Christmas, Thanksgiving, and Easter. The rest of the time I entertain casually with a buffet set up on the dining-room table. Beforehand, I clean the powder room, living room, dining room, and family room on the main floor. I trust that guests will ignore the clutter in the office and breakfast room, where all the debris from the other rooms ends up. My husband and I don't agree on this. He thinks I should clean better, while I think that too much cleaning tips the balance away from entertaining our friends.

It is my firm contention that our friends come to see us and not the state of the house. When Tony helps me clean up, the downstairs always ends up cleaner since a lot of the clutter is comprised of his sermon notes, books, and clergy magazines as well as his bill paying system that tends to occupy one entire end of the dining room table. If I exhaust myself cleaning and get too fussy about the house being perfect, I am not in a good mood to play hostess, which defeats the goal of having company. I want to be able to enjoy my guests and have them enjoy me. That is why they have come over.

I try to keep our living room free of debris for drop-in guests. The great thing about drop-ins is that you can ritually ask forgiveness for the clutter and they are obligated to be polite and pretend not to notice, since they did stop by without warning. So our living room is usually kept presentable, if only for spontaneous guests and for the door-to-door salespeople whom my husband invariably takes pity on and invites inside.

My daughter has reached the age where she and her friends desire a degree of privacy to play board games or video games or watch movies. I set up a sitting room for her with book shelves, a card table, and an old sofa with an affordable slipcover thrown over it. I pop popcorn for the movies and keep fresh fruit, bottles of water, and paper cups around. I want our home to be a place where Taylor and her friends can feel welcome to hang out. I love the sound of pounding feet running down the stairs and out of the door to the ice cream truck, then galloping back in again. Sounds like home.

Homes have always been status symbols, but the growing

wealth of college-educated Americans has meant that keeping up with the Joneses can get completely out of hand. In the Washington, D.C., area where I live, fields of mini-mansions seem to crop up overnight. Homes are enormous, each room decorated with matching furniture and coordinated window treatments. In such an environment, zit must be a challenge to remember why one needed all that space in the first place. The family is still huddled in the kitchen, only now it's an open-plan "great room."

Theoretically, with so much space it should be possible to keep such a home free of clutter. I know better. I am confident that in about a week I could have the two-story entryway of these large homes cluttered with backpacks, bicycles, and mail. Books would be stacked on either side of the couches in the formal living room. My husband would have the remnants of sermons past and the preparations for sermons future on the table in the formal dining room and the table in the great room, and he would panic at attempts to remove either mess. I would simply have farther to walk to scatter things about and a much bigger challenge finding things I had lost.

Ultimately, it is not the size or grandeur of one's house that matters, but the quality of life within. My mother made a wonderful home in a two-room rental apartment in Manhattan, a luxurious hotel apartment, a three-bedroom mini-ranch with one bathroom in Atlanta, and in her dream house with the cathedral-ceilinged living room. It was never the house that mattered. Her love and presence always made it a home.

DON'T FEEL GUILTY

Like most young women today, I was brought up with the expectation that I would someday have both a career and a family. This was the example set by my mother, who, from when I was in first grade until I went off to college, held a full-time job in education. She approached her responsibilities as blessings and opportunities rather than as burdens. Most important, she was not ruled by guilt because she was a mother who also worked outside the home.

Mother started her family early in her marriage because of misinformation from a doctor who warned her that she would have difficulty giving birth. Although she had intended to wait to have children, this concern prompted her not to delay. I was born in a small-town hospital in Thomasville, Georgia, fourteen months after her marriage to my father. While it was common practice at that time to subject the birthing mother to general anesthesia, Mother refused to be medicated, despite the protests of the nurse that it would be better for the baby.

Mother had become aware of the work and opinions of Dr. Lamaze, who believed that the extensive use of drugs was unhealthy for both mother and baby. There were no Lamaze classes or instructors in Thomasville, so she and my father read a book on the Lamaze method and practiced the exercises on their own. My father was not permitted in the hospital delivery room to coach her; when they came into the hospital with Mother in labor, she was whisked away behind closed doors. My father paced and fretted in front of the nurses' station, concerned that Mother was being left alone and unattended. He urged the nurse to check on her. "That baby's not coming, she'll scream when it's time," the nurse responded in a matter-of-fact tone. My father would not relent, though, until the nurse went into Mother's room, and found to her surprise, that Mother was fully engaged in a Lamaze breathing pattern and on the brink of delivery. The doctor was called, and he arrived in time to catch the baby.

Confidence in her own judgment and a belief in her own methods were characteristic of Mother's approach to child-rearing. From the beginning, her experience was that the experts had only so much to offer, and their opinions should be viewed with a healthy skepticism. She would make her own decisions about what was best for her children and not feel guilty about it. She would not conform to someone else's view about what was best for her family unless it rang true based on her own experience.

As she raised her children, many of Mother's actions ran contrary to the instructions of the experts of the time. She breast-fed her babies, although baby formula was then being touted as the perfect, scientific nutrition for infants. She didn't force her children to adhere to strict feeding and sleeping schedules. In her view, babies were simply a part of life and with some adjustments, the baby would eat when she was hungry, sleep when she was sleepy, and eventually come to match the rhythms of the family. One of the many advantages of breast-feeding was that it made the baby far more portable— no heavy glass bottles had to be sterilized or carried around. When I was a baby, Mother took me everywhere—to church or on a car trip to California with her husband's parents. She parented with an easygoing pragmatism.

As had my grandmother, my mother pursued her educational goals even after her children were born. The summer I turned three, my mother was going to summer school to earn her master's degree in education. It was not easy to study with an active toddler racing around the house, so she sent me to spend six weeks with my grandparents, first in New Orleans and then to Marion. While I was in New Orleans, my grandmother nursed me through the measles, reading me stories and applying layers of calamine lotion. Mother had total confidence that my grandmother could handle the measles.

During the civil rights movement, my mother at times would be overwhelmed with a desire to be a part of the marches and demonstrations that occurred. We had a distant cousin, Betty Lipscombe, who was a nursing student in Atlanta. From time to time, Mother would call her or one of our babysitters to stay with the children for a few days while she went to St. Augustine or Selma to participate in a demonstration. She contributed so much behind the scenes; sometimes she just had to be on the front line.

Once, when I was still single and childless, I was in the kitchen helping my mother make dinner when my brother came in and began complaining about a trip Mother was taking to the board meeting of the Children's Defense Fund. Bo was in grade school and very articulate and forceful in making his case for abandonment and chiding her for leaving him alone. Mother wasn't having it. She calmly explained the arrangements she had made for him, where he would be staying, his transportation to and from school, and when she would return home. He listened sulkily and left the room. Mother turned to me and said, "Don't let your children make you feel guilty. You are the parent and you decide what's best. If you respond to your children out of guilt, you begin to resent them and that's not healthy."

My brother and sisters and I never doubted that our mother loved us dearly. She responded to us from love and from her sense of responsibility, not out of guilt. She was able to set limits and preserve her own space to be the person that she was in addition to being our mother.

Taylor was born after I had been in the workforce for nearly a decade. I was very comfortable with my professional identity and I expected to maintain a fairly relaxed attitude toward my newborn. But I was completely unprepared for the overwhelming sense of joy I felt when I held her. She looked up at me with an incredible expression of trust, and I knew I would do just about anything to make her happy.

After ten months at home with her, I had a wonderful job opportunity and I went back to work. My daughter did very well in daycare. Taylor was very friendly, but had no young siblings at home to play with and she enjoyed the friends she made. I selected an established, well-run program with a union and benefits for the staff. Taylor's first teacher had been at the Center for nine years.

When my daughter was twenty-one months old, I had to attend a week-long biannual meeting of the United Church of Christ as part of my work. I took Taylor to stay with my mother in Atlanta. Ironically, one of the positions being debated by the church delegates at the meeting was whether the issue of separation of church and state should take precedence over a daycare bill then pending in the Congress in which some provisions would have given public dollars to religious institutions to provide childcare. I was intensely disturbed by the abstract nature of the debate and I took the position that the care of children was more important than the First Amendment. I became very emotional, and realized that I missed my daughter. I knew she was fine with my mother and I was pleased that they had a chance to be together, but I was not fine being away from Taylor for so long. I wasn't experiencing feelings of guilt, but of loneliness.

When Taylor was small, a good friend with a baby near Taylor's age organized a group we called the Mother's Club. We met at someone's house once a month, to share the joys and trials of parenting. Most of us were women who had our children after first establishing a career track record, and we were struggling with how to balance our own needs, our obligation to provide for our family, and the needs of our children. Most women in the group continued with their careers, but moved off the fast track. One woman who had been in research transferred out of the lab when she ruined an experiment because of an emergency call from her child's daycare center. Another simply reduced her hours.

The Mother's Club once had a fascinating session with a local psychologist about the balance between career and parenting. Dr. Carlotta Miles cautioned us not to delegate to others too much of the everyday responsibilities of childcare, and she encouraged simple things like driving the car pool at least once a week and avoiding working overtime or habitually staying late at the office. She believed it was important for family members to share all the days events over dinner. She basically confirmed what most of us already understood and really wanted to do for our children and ourselves. We experienced stress in our complicated lives, but we also knew that we were privileged to have the kind of options and alternatives that we enjoyed.

My husband and I agreed together to have one child. Since he had two children from his previous marriage, he asked, only half-jokingly, that he have a break between day-care and a nursing home. With the demanding careers we each have, we are better able to provide emotional support for one. I cherish the experience of raising my daughter and try to limit the amount of time I must delegate her care to others.

One of the most exciting phases of my career was the time I spent as Chief of Staff to Cynthia McKinney, a dynamic new member of Congress. My work required long hours on Capitol Hill as legislation was debated late into the night. Often, it seemed that I didn't see my daughter in the daylight. After two years, I had had enough. I loved the feeling of consequence at my job, the meetings at the White House and receptions at the Capitol, and the sense of making a difference in national policy. But I needed to make a difference in my daughter's life and I wasn't as involved there as I wanted to be. I will never regret those years on the Hill and I don't feel guilty about them, but I made the right choice to leave.

Through my mother's teachings and the personal example of the life she lived, I learned that it was all right to balance my need for professional expression with the needs of my family. Every choice I have made to defer my career goals has been made not out of guilt, but from a genuine desire to grant myself the pleasure of hands-on parenting. It is a gift to be able to parent from the strength of my love and commitment. Sometimes I gaze fondly at my daughter and she looks back at me and smiles. "You really love me, don't you," she says.

TELL THE TRUTH

My mother and her siblings were raised to tell the truth. If their mother, Miss Idella, had any suspicions of their wrong-doing, she would preface her questions regarding telltale signs of mischief with, "Don't let me find out from somebody else!" The implication was that punishment would be infinitely more severe if there was an attempt at concealment. Given the tiny size of the town of Marion, it was highly unlikely that any mischief would go unnoticed by some adult who was sure to tell Miss Idella, eventually. For parenting purposes, small towns are great places.

From her sister Cora, my mother learned a wonderful

lesson about the importance of honesty. Miss Idella was active on a number of committees and clubs, and she regularly hosted meetings of her women's club. Early in the morning, she would begin the preparations for the club meeting, including attractively arranging perfectly fashioned finger sandwiches and slices of her famous pound cake on trays. Once she had to go out briefly before the meeting was to begin, and she sternly admonished her five children not to touch the food. The charming sandwiches in squares and triangles made from store-bought bread with the crusts removed were extremely tempting, and Bill, the oldest, succumbed first. He decided he would just take one. But before long, the lovely trays were in shambles. Cora had resisted, knowing that her mother would be furious if anything happened to the food she had so lovingly prepared.

Sure enough, Miss Idella returned home and immediately looked at her trays. She was livid. She knew five culprits with motive and opportunity and she lined the children up to dispense spankings to each. She started with Bill and worked down in age to Cora, who finally spoke up for herself. She said, "Mother, I really didn't touch any of the party food. It isn't that I didn't want it, but I didn't have any." Cora was spared with no questions asked.

My mother was the youngest, and her big brother offered to take her punishment. But she had known better and she would get her punishment. Cora reaped the benefits of having a reputation for honesty, and Mother always remembered that if you were known as an honest and truthful person, you would be believed, even in suspicious circumstances.

Miss Idella did make allowances for situational ethics. When my mother was a little girl she would accompany Miss Idella during the summers to Montgomery where she was completing her degree. It was very costly for her to do this and it was a measure of my grandmother's commitment to education that she was determined to earn her college degree. They used the bus to travel back and forth to Alabama State College. At seven, my mother was small for her age and children under six traveled for free, so to save the precious pennies, grandmother instructed my mother not to read the signs aloud. She told the bus driver, "She's not six." Later, she pointed out to my mother that that was true; she was not six, she was seven.

Miss Idella hadn't told a lie, although the literal truth was misleading. She was conscious of violating an important principle in front of her young daughter and she wanted to make it clear that she did not consider it a lie. It was also true that because of segregation, black passengers did not receive the same value for their fare as did white passengers, since blacks had to sit at the back and stand as long as a white passenger needed a seat. So my grandmother may have felt that she was simply getting full value for the fare she paid. My grandmother could get very defensive when this story was told; it represented a conflict within her of deeply held values.

I learned at a relatively early age how deeply my mother valued truth. She had been given a lovely decorative plate as a wedding present and it sat on display on the breakfront in the dining room. I knew I was not to touch it. Of course, that made it the more alluring and one day when my mother was out of the house, I took the plate down to play with it. It was much heavier than I anticipated, and it immediately slipped from my hands and crashed to the floor. Frantically gathering pieces, I realized it was broken beyond repair. I sat the fragments back on the breakfront, and went outside to play as if I had never touched it.

When my mother returned, it did not take her long to notice the broken plate. Without yelling or accusing me, she asked if I knew what had happened to it. No one had seen me with the plate, and I could have denied knowledge, but I had been raised to tell the truth and I confessed. I braced myself for my mother's anger, but instead her arm went around my shoulder in a hug. "Accidents happen," she said. "I appreciate your honesty." She was so pleased that she chose to reinforce my positive action rather than punish me.

The importance of truth has been a touchstone in the way my sister Lisa has raised her own children, although she has no recollection of a specific instance or lesson about it. It is just something she's always known, and she makes it a point to demonstrate that lying will not be tolerated in her home. Recently, her young son came home from day camp where he had been encouraged to swim every day. When asked whether he had taken his swimming lessons, Kemet nodded and quickly changed the subject. Later, Lisa found his stone-dry towel and swim trunks in his backpack. When Lisa's husband, Douglas, came home, together they gave their son one more chance to tell the truth. When Kemet assured his father that he had indeed gone swimming, Lisa and Douglas took away his video game privileges. By my thinking it was a fairly harmless lie, but Lisa maintains a zero-tolerance policy.

While Lisa follows my grandmother's formula of punishment that was weighted more heavily if the offender is also caught in a lie, I take a different approach with my daughter by making it easy for her to tell the truth. I try to maintain an open mind and refrain from accusing. But I am not always successful, and she is quick to point out when she has been unjustly accused.

Thanks to my mother, I am a terrible liar. I was conditioned to believe the truth would be rewarded and I cannot lie with a straight face. I went to college in Pennsylvania where the legal drinking age was twenty-one. In Georgia, where I was from, the drinking age was eighteen, and I thought Pennsylvania was being unreasonable, if not unjust. The sales clerks at the time wouldn't demand identification from purchasers of alcohol, but occasionally they would ask your age. When asked the question directly, I found myself stammering, unable to tack on the extra two years. My friends insisted that I stay in the car: "One look at your face, Andrea, and they'll know we're underage." I cannot say that this policy prevented me from drinking socially when I was under twenty-one, but now that I am a parent I am in full support of a twenty-one-year-old drinking age (and an eighteen-year-old driving age, too, for that matter).

Somehow, in our culture, the inability to lie is seen as a weakness. In my training as a lawyer, this was a major professional disadvantage for me. The ability to conceal the truth is a highly valued skill in tough negotiations, both civil and criminal. I found the adversarial structure of conflict resolution in law to be counterproductive to solving the real problems that people had. When sentencing was the only real issue, I could argue convincingly for a judgment that would allow my client probation or drug treatment. But when I had doubts about a client's role in a crime, I had real difficulty with representation.

Our cherished cultural myths include George Washington as a boy chopping down the cherry tree saying, "I cannot tell a lie." Comic book and movie hero Superman is supposed to fight for "truth, justice, and the American way." But these are values we have gotten away from because winning—and winning at all costs—has become an all-important goal.

Yet there is so much power in truth. The civil rights movement was based on the understanding that confronting American society with the truth of the injustice of segregation could create change. Civil disobedience was used to illustrate and highlight the effect of segregation with carefully planned marches and sit-ins, actions which were against the law. Mohandas Gandhi's philosophy of nonviolent disobedience required that in disobeying even unjust laws, the nonviolent activist must be prepared to accept responsibility and the punishment for his or her actions. The moral stance of responsibility must underlie all nonviolent action. Even the unjustness of the law or the unjustness of a politically motivated investigation does not eliminate the need to accept responsibility and consequences. Gandhi titled his autobiography *My Experiments with Truth*, referring to the literal translation of Gandhi's word for nonviolence: "truth-force." He spoke truth to power, accepting the consequences of that truth.

Truth can overcome injustice and promote healing. It is an essential element of genuine relationships and it is a fundamental religious value. Truth is so simple, yet is so often breached. In matters large and small, family affairs or affairs of state, truth builds trust, and the absence of truth destroys it.

When I was a college student, I attended an open house with a number of young professionals in their twenties. The hosts were a couple I didn't know very well, but they were friends of a classmate and her husband. I was troubled by improper advances made toward me by our host, which I deflected, and I later asked our common friend whether our peers believed in fidelity in marriage. He replied that the danger in infidelity was that once you cheated on your wife, you could never trust her again. I understood, immediately.

We cannot expect others to exemplify higher character than we ourselves are willing to display. If I do not tell the truth, I will cease to expect truth from others, and I will suspect others of lying even when they are not. Telling the truth allows you to expect the best of yourself and of others.

DO YOUR BEST

Lodged forever in my memory is a childhood jingle that I associate with girls' breathlessness and jumping rope:

Good, better, best,
never let it rest,
'til your good is better
and your better, best.

I don't know where I first heard this, but it wouldn't surprise me if it was my mother's idea, a more constructive jump-rope mantra in her mind than "John and Mary sitting in a tree, k-i-s-s-i-n-g." Easygoing about many things, Mother was firm on academic matters. Her children would do their very best.

Her high standards for education came from her own family and from the dedicated teachers at Lincoln School. She never forgot her second-grade teacher, Julia Macbeth, whom she truly loved. Although Mother was small for her age, she had been sent to second grade directly after kindergarten because she could read. Mrs. Macbeth transformed what could have been an overwhelming experience into a delight.

Despite the presence of segregation around them, the teachers at Lincoln were determined to prepare their students to compete with the best and the brightest, to defy popular stereotypes of black inferiority. In the process, everyone was pushed to his or her limits. The tradition at Lincoln was so strong that in the 1950s, educator Dr. Horace Mann Bond found that a remarkable number of black Ph.D.'s or their parents had attended Lincoln. As the keynote speaker for the Lincolnite Reunion in Marion in the early 1980s, my mother spoke lovingly of her school and teachers. The Lincoln legacy was first a good education; second, a strong sense of self-assurance, confidence, and pride; third, a commitment to others; and fourth, personal ambition.

Herself a graduate of Lincoln, Miss Idella reinforced these standards and expectations with her three daughters. Having been raised on the dawn-to-dusk schedule of a working farm, Idella was a demanding task-master for her family.

The youngest child, my mother, did not have the full range of chores and responsibilities visited on the eldest children. It made it all the more notable and less excusable if the chores she did have were not performed to her mother's satisfaction.

After school, my mother took the family cow, Pretty Gal, out to graze on fresh grass. She had to take care that the field she chose had no bitter weed or onions for the cow to eat. If the breakfast milk tasted of onions, Mother would face the accusing stares of her siblings and Miss Idella. My mother would keep one eye on her Wonder Woman comic book and the other on the cow. On Saturdays, Mother and her sister Cora were responsible for cleaning the backyard. Debris was to be picked up, playthings, projects, and balls put away, leaves and pine needles raked, an area of hardpacked clay swept. No matter how pleased Cora and my mother were with the successful completion of their task, Miss Idella could always find something they had missed. Any chore Idella required would be reviewed with a critical eye. "Well, what about *this?*" she would say. Consequently, my mother developed an abiding internal critic, while at the same time she pushed herself to take on extraordinary responsibility and challenges.

One of Mother's remarkable challenges was to make my father's career possible. In her early thirties, she had three children, a full-time teaching job, and a husband who was always on the road. Recently, when my father spent the day with my younger sister Paula and her two young sons, he realized the tremendous weight that had rested on my mother's shoulders as he traveled with Martin Luther King in pursuit of American civil rights. Like my mother, Paula is a teacher and her husband travels constantly for the NAACP. My father experienced a huge wave of concern for his youngest daughter and the stress she must feel managing her family and her career.

Ann Richards, former governor of Texas, once said of Ginger Rogers: "Ginger did everything Fred Astaire did, only backwards in high heels." That was my mother in the 1960s. When it came to her husband, her children at home, and her kids at school, she would dance backward in high heels to fulfill her responsibility.

One of the gifts that made this possible was Mother's ability to focus her energy on life's most important activities. As she had done with Pretty Gal, Mother identified her core responsibility and her main goal and she directed her best efforts in that area. She might arrive at her job late after packing three kids of her own off to school, but once there she was the best teacher the children would ever have, attentive, caring, and creative. After a full day of demanding work, she could always rally herself to entertain the company that my father brought home for dinner—often he'd call her just as they were leaving his office or a meeting and already on the way home. She gave her best to these leaders and foot soldiers of the Movement, putting comfort food on the table and keeping a charming smile on her face. It was not her way to complain; her inner critic simply instructed her to work harder.

As Mother reflected on her upbringing and the ways in which she would raise her own children, it was never her intention to transmit the messages of her inner critic to her own children. She felt that Miss Idella had been too harsh a taskmaster and had been much too sparing in her praise. Mother made a big effort to praise her children's accomplishments, our chores around the house, our artwork or creative projects, and our positive behavior. But in education, however, standards could not be too high.

Before my younger sisters had even started school, Mother held summer school at our house and taught us to read with phonics workbooks she made herself. She bought oversized cream-colored posterboard and drew pictures and symbols to illustrate sounds and words. Each workbook was tied together with yarn and designed at our respective reading level. Our friends could come and work with us, but we could not go out to play until we had completed the assignments Mother set out for us. We were expected to excel in school and work to our own ability, regardless of what else the class was doing. In second grade, I received perfect scores except in conduct. The teacher complained to my mother that I would complete my work and then begin to disturb the other children. To Mother the answer was simple—"Give her more work," she told my teacher.

Once, when my mother discovered that my brother was behind in his fourth-grade spelling assignments, she canceled his activities and took away his phone privileges for the weekend. She supervised while Bo worked Friday, Saturday, and Sunday afternoon to catch up. Only for church and Sunday School was he permitted to go out of the house. Bo went to school Monday morning with half a semester's spelling assignments completed to Mother's satisfaction.

Mother's expectation of academic performance was even stronger when I was in high school. She took A's for granted and only commented on the B's. She knew that the B's did not represent my true abilities, except in math. In trigonometry, each test came with a bonus question which required the ability to take everything that had been taught and apply it to the next step. I could memorize the formulas, but I never understood them. As a result, I could never answer the bonus question correctly. Despite her rigorous standards, Mother understood that this wasn't for lack of trying and that it was not an area where she could help me.

When it came to other academic subjects, though, she was not so tolerant. Among the requirements for graduation for girls in the Atlanta Public Schools was Home Economics. My girlfriends and I thought this course was a huge waste of our time. We had learned more than we wanted to know on this subject from our mothers and grandmothers. This class was supposed to teach meal planning and preparation, table settings, household budgeting, and home decorating. In the decorating segment, our teacher spent an inordinate amount of time on window treatments. This was an era of heavy, multi-layered floor-length drapes. I can say now, with pride, that I have never had any such thing in my home.

Our final project was to prepare a scrapbook of our dream home. It was to include a layout of the house and photos from magazines illustrating the decoration of each room and a description using the proper terminology for the fabrics, furniture, and of course, window treatments. In my twelfth-grade mind, this was a project better suited to fifth grade. The Sunday night before the project was due, I was sitting at the dining-room table putting on the finishing touches when my mother happened to look over my shoulder. She frowned thoughtfully as she looked through the scrapbook, and pointed at the cover. "This is not very creative," she said. "You can do better." She made suggestions and before I could protest, the look on her face communicated that I was not going to be allowed to turn in the project in its existing form.

I went back over the scrapbook, painstakingly rewrote the copy for each page, and made a new cover. The result was an A-plus. I am certain that my original effort would have produced an A, but Mother knew that I was capable of getting that "plus."

Later, at Swarthmore College, I was grateful for my mother's high expectations. The work was far more rigorous—

and interesting—than anything I had done in high school. Entire books had to be read between classes, tests required long essays rather than multiple-choice answers, and each class required a research paper. Challenged to do my best, I was never bored. I was prepared because my mother had so often required that I do more than my teachers requested.

My own daughter knows that I have very high expectations of her academic performance. Her father and I have made financial sacrifices to place her in the best possible school, and she hears daily that school is her job, her responsibility. One evening I was signing her test papers, as her teachers require, and I came across a good grade on a geography test. Taylor bragged that she hadn't even studied for it. I looked at her sternly and said, "Then this grade does not represent your best work."

A long conversation ensued in which my daughter argued that she did better than some girls who did study, and I responded that I was not concerned about other girls' grades; I was concerned that *her* grades represented her best effort. It was possible, but unlikely, that a grade less than an A might represent Taylor's best work, I told her. As a general principle, any grade less than an A meant she had failed to do her best. My daughter became very quiet, and I haven't heard any more about not studying for tests.

I want Taylor to develop the habit of working to her potential. Her future, I believe, depends on her ability to learn and master new skills and information. The world of her adulthood will be an unforgiving place for the poorly educated. While I encourage her studies I have tried to balance criticism with praise for her accomplishments. She demonstrates a delightful creativity as an artist and writer, and one of her poems was used as her school's holiday card. But every gift requires practice and discipline to achieve its best expression. Taylor is known for her enthusiasm and I would like her to be known for her diligence, as well.

As a result, my daughter can feel pressured by my expectations. Recently, she caught me by surprise when she defended her school work by saying, "I'm not perfect like you, okay?" I responded to her that I certainly didn't consider myself perfect. Far from it. But I recall viewing my own mother as being nearly perfect. I never saw her insecurities or heard her internal critic. For a child who is still mastering many of the basic skills of modern life, a parent's adeptness may seem like perfection. I want my daughter to appreciate the years of practice, study, and trial and error that result in my level of competence. Of course I am capable of a tremendous number of skills that my daughter has yet to master. But there are areas where Taylor has applied herself and developed skills superior to mine—in art, softball, and music, for example.

I reassured her that my demands and my expectations are a sign of my love and respect for her and her abilities. I don't push her because she is a poor student, but because she is a good student who could be better. She has many talents, but each requires hard work on her part to fully emerge and develop. Ultimately, Taylor must develop her own internal quality standard, one that allows for risk-taking and honest mistakes and acknowledges superior effort. I'll continue to provide that balance until her own internal voice begins to hum.

A GIRL'S BEST FRIEND
IS HER MOTHER

My mother raised her daughters as if we were birds perched in her open palm. There were no bonds to confine us as we grew. She made every effort to enable our choices and our aspirations. She was our champion, our companion, and our friend as we matured. Our appreciation of her strength and goodness increased as our understanding and experience expanded over time.

My grandmother Idella Childs raised three smart and beautiful daughters whom she never allowed to be cowed or to accept limits on their dreams. In the 1940s, as each girl graduated from high school, Miss Idella encouraged her to leave the South to attend a small liberal-arts college established by the Church of the Brethren in Indiana. When World War II ended, the oldest and boldest of the three sisters, Norma Louise, went to Berlin to work as a social worker with displaced families. Although Norma lived in the city's American-controlled sector, it must have been frightening to her parents to know that she was in a country where people had been mercilessly killed for deviating from some fictional Aryan ideal. Fran and Cecil Thomas, Christian teachers who had worked in the Lincoln School in Marion and who were running the displaced-persons project, wanted Norma to come to Germany as a living example of the tragedy of Hitler's ideology. Precisely because of the Nazi ideology, the Thomases wanted an integrated staff for their project.

During her sophomore year in college, my mother wrote home to share with her parents an opportunity for her to travel to eastern Europe with a Christian Youth Camp. My grandmother not only gave her permission but wrote Mother's brother, Norman, Jr., to encourage him to send money to his sister for her trip. From various sources, Miss Idella pulled together $150. She wrote that, regretfully, she and my grandfather would be unable to drive Jean from Indiana to Quebec to meet the freighter ship that would take the students across the Atlantic. Miss Idella was pleased, and perhaps relieved, that my father rearranged his summer to join the camp as well. The students virtually camped out in the ship's hold during the Atlantic crossing. As the only African-Americans in the group, Mother and my father agreed to be sent to different villages, demonstrating, by integrating their work teams, that American values were the antithesis of Nazi racism.

Miss Idella raised unconventional girls who resisted conformity to the racial and gender norms of their era. She sent them to Manchester College, where they would learn to relate to white people outside the boundaries and restrictions of segregation. All three of her daughters completed their college degrees before they married, rather than dropping out to put husbands through school as so many young women did in the period after World War II. Idella was determined that her daughters would be college graduates.

There was a special relationship among Miss Idella and her daughters. Her eldest took up residence in New York City, but she faithfully called her mother and talked for hours each week. The middle daughter, Cora, married and took up residence in Uniontown, the nearest town to Marion. Cora was very much her mother's daughter, a missionary to her own community. Together, mother and daughter sustained Marion's small, but historic Congregational Church. In one of many collaborations, Cora and Miss Idella organized a successful political campaign to elect Cora's daughter-in-law Clerk of Records for Perry County.

My grandmother had encouraged her girls to pursue the unlikely and test the outer ranges of the possible. She refused to overprotect them or undermine their adventures with her own anxieties. In so doing, she allowed them to become more than she ever could have imagined.

My mother, as well, gave her daughters permission to push the edges of the envelope. From what I knew of my grandmother's philosophical legacy, I knew I could expect that my mother would tolerate a fair amount of adventurousness on my part. During the summer of my father's first political campaign, when I was fifteen, one of my oldest friends invited me to go with her to Rock Hill, South Carolina, for her cousin's wedding. This was going to be three days of food, festivities, and fun, and I was eager to go. But I also knew that my parents expected me to spend the weekend with them attending campaign events. I packed my bag and jumped in my friend Jennifer's old Mercedes. We hit the interstate. When we reached the South Carolina line, I called my mother and told her where I was. She tried to sound stern and warned me that I would face punishment when I returned, but I thought I heard amusement in her voice. When I came home I argued that my parents had known where I was, they had known the girl I was with for ten years, and they were aware that her parents were members of our church and that we were at a family event. But I took full responsibility for leaving on a trip without permission. I was grounded for a month, which meant I couldn't go out with my friends, but I followed my parents to half a dozen campaign events every day. Mother was impressed with my sense of adventure and independence. I was disciplined, but without anger and not in a manner that rejected my spiritedness.

When my youngest sister, Lisa, wanted to take the boys' class in mechanical drawing at school rather than the girls' home economics class, Mother supported her choice, taking her request to the principal. As a result, Lisa became the first girl in our high school to take mechanical drawing. Later, she earned a degree in electrical engineering.

When it was time for college, my mother continued Miss Idella's tradition. It was understood that we girls would go to school away from home, although there were excellent colleges in Atlanta. I went to Swarthmore, in a suburb of Philadelphia; Lisa went to Purdue in Indiana and Howard in Washington, D.C.; Paula attended Duke in North Carolina. When my youngest sister decided to go to Uganda as a missionary after one of its civil wars, my mother gave her blessing and my parents helped raise the funds she needed for the trip.

It was after I graduated from college that I truly began to appreciate my mother as a friend and confidante. She was a wonderful listener who would let me talk out issues and would refrain from offering advice unless it was solicited. Her advice was tempered with wisdom, and she was always ready with a compliment and slow with criticism. Her presence was empowering: she was a strong woman, but never overbearing. And she was willing to learn from me as well as teach me.

In college, I took every women's history class offered. Women's history was a new and somewhat controversial discipline, and the texts we studied revealed a complex struggle for women's equality beginning in the early nineteenth century. My mother affirmed my interest, reading all my course texts herself and using examples from them in her speeches. She particularly liked to quote Sojourner Truth's speech "Ain't I a Woman," given from the balcony, rather than the podium, of a convention on women's suffrage.

Mother trusted her children to make our own decisions and our own mistakes. She was not motivated by guilt or control, but related to us instead with respect. No matter how she worried about some of our actions, she did not criticize our decisions. We tested her, though, with every extreme. My youngest sister began dating her now husband in the summer, and married him the following June. When I raised with mother my concerns over whether Paula had known this man long enough to make such a decision, her response was, "It's her decision." My middle sister, Lisa, dated the same man off and on for nearly five years. One Christmas, he had given her a diamond solitaire necklace. I began to tease them, saying, "These diamonds are the right idea, but the wrong setting." My mother hushed me, saying it was none of my business. She had an unwavering conviction that no one had the right to direct another person's important decisions. The one who had to live with the consequences was fully entitled to her choice, no matter what her family thought.

I was unaware of how much my mother worried about the men I dated. In retrospect, they were an eclectic group. Anyone she met was treated with friendly courtesy and once they were gone, she refrained from any sort of critique. It was only after I married that she let on that she was relieved by my final choice.

Acceptance and support were my mother's gifts to her children. Whenever I called on the telephone, she always seemed interested in what I had to say. We talked about situations at work as well as social and family matters. When I moved to Washington, Mother came to spend time with me and my friends, chatting and going out to dinner. When I was ready to marry, she accepted my choice without question and organized a beautiful wedding. When my daughter was born, Mother managed to be in town the night I went into labor and remained with me for a week afterward. If a friend is someone who is always there when you need her, a dear companion who loves you when you are at your best and when you are not, no one could have been a better friend to me throughout my life than my mother.

Mother's ability to be nonjudgmental allowed the two of us to be friends. She did not try to control my life or the lives of my sisters and brother, or push us toward a direction she thought more appropriate than the one we had chosen for ourselves. I could go to her for help, confident that she would remain in a supportive role rather than trying to dominate. Because she was so enabling, I felt no need to reject her or rebel to assert my independence. She was a trusted collaborator with me and my siblings in the building of our lives.

My sisters share my feelings about our mother. One Mother's Day, after Lisa and I had graduated from college and law school and had been working long enough to have discretionary income, we wanted to do something particularly special for Mother. She was not inclined to spend a lot of money on herself or her clothes, so we wanted to give her the kind of classic suit that she would never buy on her own. For years we had watched our mother wear inexpensive dresses to national and international events where other women were wearing thousand-dollar outfits with comparably expensive jewelry. We were determined to give her a suit that she could wear to a board meeting of the Junior League or to address a national convention and have the women present admire her clothes.

We went to the designer department at Neiman-Marcus and explained to the saleswoman what we wanted to do. She brought out several beautiful knit suits. Lisa tried them for fit, although the saleswoman assured us that Mother could certainly exchange any outfit we purchased for something else.

We paid $900 for the perfect Mother's Day suit. It was

so expensive we had to ask the saleswoman to divide the bill between our two credit cards. It was not something that our mother would have expected us to do. But we needed to give Mother something extraordinary to acknowledge how we felt about her care and support. The suit became a staple of her wardrobe.

I share with my own daughter truth and a belief in all her glorious possibilities. It is true, as she so often points out, that many things about our society are not fair. We talk about the nature of that unfairness, the history of the exclusion of women from sports, careers, and civic and political decision-making. We talk about strategies women have used to overcome unfairness and barriers. Sometimes, in my eagerness to share what I have learned, I go over her head or I explain something she isn't ready to face yet. It isn't healthy to force feed truth any more than to reject it. I want Taylor to believe in herself and her ability to overcome obstacles, even as she perceives their existence. Ultimately, justice and fairness will prevail.

When popular culture depicts mothers as overbearing, smothering, and stifling, I cringe. The temptation to coddle and protect is certainly there. It is the negative side of the security and stability mothers can provide. Demanding social conformity from a daughter or trying to shape her into her mother's vision of what a girl or woman should be invites resentment and rebellion. In that context, a daughter must reject her mother in order to be herself. But my mother's way was to be a partner in our growth, exposing us to options and helping us reach the goals we set.

My daughter is still in the phase of girlhood where she believes in herself and her possibilities. Her personality is characterized by tremendous enthusiasm and zest for life. I have to help her use her wings, while teaching her not to fly headlong into trees. If I succeed in giving her the space to grow in the security of my love and regard, my reward will be a strong, intelligent, and admirable woman, and a lifelong friend.

KNOW YOUR HISTORY

My grandmother taught social studies to countless children in Marion, and her students learned about the accomplishments of black Americans: scientists like the Wizard of Tuskegee and George Washington Carver; educators like Booker T. Washington and W. E. B. Du Bois; abolitionists like Frederick Douglass and Harriet Tubman; and poets such as Phillis Wheatley and Paul Laurence Dunbar. My grandmother took on the responsibility for preserving African-American history in Marion, placing both the Congregational church and the site of the Lincoln School on the national register of historic places.

She hoped that by preserving the past, she would inspire future generations to aspire to achieve comparable goals.

When my parents returned from their first European trip with slides of sites in Berlin and Rome, they were surprised by the depth of information my grandmother had on these monuments and cathedrals. My parents knew the names of the sites, but though she had never traveled overseas, my grandmother knew their full story and significance. History was her passion.

It's no wonder that Idella raised my mother with a sense of her own family's history and a respect for its importance. When she had her own children, my mother read to us the poetry of Paul Laurence Dunbar and continued the tradition of supplementing our standard history curriculum with stories from African-American history. She wanted us to have an appreciation and understanding of the role African-Americans played in shaping America, the contributions they made that were ignored or downplayed in contemporary school books. For example, our 1960s Georgia history textbook described Reconstruction as a time of suffering, and the Freedmen's Bureau as a corrupt failure with no mention of the churches and schools that endure to this day, established by and for the freed slaves.

Influenced by my grandmother's delight in history and my mother's sense of its importance, I chose it as my college major. I was fortunate to study history with Dr. Kathryn Morgan, who earned one of the first doctorates in oral history from the University of Pennsylvania. Her classes were very popular with feminist students, who were interested to learn how to use nontraditional sources to explore the contributions of women in the development of America. Traditional history recorded the actions and views of the dominant males in a society; Dr. Morgan's students were curious about the activities of factory workers, laborers, and domestic servants, and the efforts by these classes of people to address their social status.

For one of my college papers, my grandmother told the story of one of our African ancestors, a princess from East Africa, probably Madagascar or Ethiopia. According to the story, she was sold into slavery by an uncle in order to clear his title to the throne. One of my cousins, Arthur Childs, was able to verify that indeed this woman had been called "Princess" and she was treated with deference by the family who owned her.

Whether this story was literally true, it psychically sustained my ancestors during slavery and inspired their constant search for freedom. The granddaughter of the Princess, Patsy Freeman, was able to purchase her freedom and move to Ohio in the early 1800s. James Childs, my direct ancestor, purchased his own freedom in the years preceding the Civil War. It is a part of my family's oral history that the fair-skinned James was the son of his owner, which would also account for his status as a free person of color before the Civil War.

I found talking with my grandmother about these traditions to be inspirational in a way I could not have predicted. The continuous flow of family and history gave me a sense of place. I had an incredible legacy to live up to, one which would sustain me throughout my life.

In the mid-1980s, my mother's interest in her African origins and the princess from East Africa was stirred by Dr. Asa Hilliard, a professor at Georgia State University, who is a proponent of the controversial view that Egyptian civilization is African in origin, rather than Greek or Mediterranean. In 1989 Mother accompanied Dr. Hilliard on one of his educational tours through Egypt's tombs and pyramids, and saw firsthand the symbols and artifacts that formed the evidence he used to support his theories. The trip was strenuous and intellectually challenging, and Mother was tremendously excited by what she learned. She believed that, reclaimed as an African civilization, Egypt would serve as a source of pride and inspiration to contemporary African-Americans.

My mother firmly believed that it was important to know this history and the whole history of African-Americans, and she worked to make that knowledge accessible to children and young people. A longtime supporter of the arts, my mother had also worked with the Martin Luther King Center for Nonviolent Social Change to develop programs to explain the civil rights movement to young people, but she came to believe that was not sufficient. The civil rights movement needed to be understood in its larger context, as a recent stage of a four-hundred-year tradition of resistance to injustice in the Americas.

Mother was pleased to respond to an invitation to join the board of a small museum called the APEX—the African-American Panoramic Experience. The vision of the APEX was to build a museum that allowed children to feel as if they were experiencing history. A sense of their place in the world and pride in the long history of people of African descent would, Mother hoped, inspire black children—especially those who were underprivileged—to dream of life's possibilities. The stories of accomplished African-Americans with which she had been raised had helped give Mother confidence that she, too, could achieve. She believed the APEX could do the same for another generation of children.

Gathering support was not an easy task. Mother was confronted with skepticism regarding the need and purpose for such a museum. The head of a major Atlanta-based foundation was rude and insulting when she met with him to gain financial support for the APEX. She was so shaken by the hostility of his response that, despite her characteristic persistence, she could not bring herself to meet with him again.

Mother persevered on other fronts. She went to Congressman John Lewis to request special funding for the APEX. She pounded the hard marble floors of Capitol Hill wearing gold-and-silver tennis shoes. She pleaded her case to members of Congress on the Appropriations Committee and to Chairman Yates of the subcommittee that considered the APEX proposal. In a meeting with Art Blank of Home Depot, she was so persuasive that he ended up giving the APEX $25,000 more than had been requested.

Mother revitalized the museum's board, calling each member personally to remind him or her of meetings. She also supported the museum's director in his refusal to accept funding that required him to advertise alcohol and tobacco products. Ironically, some of the most generous corporate support for the arts and humanities comes from alcohol and tobacco companies. But the vision of the APEX was to communicate to young people a sense of the sweep of history. It was a message that Mother agreed must not be associated with the dangerous habits of smoking cigarettes and drinking malt liquor.

While the total vision of the APEX has yet to be realized, busloads of school children enter the museum every day. Once inside, the good-natured noise turns to quiet awe when the presentations begin. Through the APEX the most underprivileged black child learns that his history did not begin in a ghetto and it will not end there. My mother believed that when children and adults know and understand their own history, it changes their perception of the possibilities for their own lives.

When my daughter was in third grade, her class was given an exercise on identity, especially ethnic identity, as a number of the girls had family roots in other cultures. I took that exercise as an opportunity to sit with Taylor and share the varied background of our family and the common theme that ties us together: commitment to family, church, and school. I wrote Taylor a long letter describing the churches started or sustained by her ancestors on both her parents' lines—her father is a third-generation Congregational minister; there is a church in North Carolina named for her great-grandmother; and even her grandmother Kathryn Turrentine was licensed to preach and train Christian educators. I wanted Taylor to understand that she came from people whose first impulse when slavery ended was to build churches and schools. I wanted her to see her family's long-held core values and traditions, and to place herself in the context of those traditions. Fortunately, we know the facts of our history going back to the Reconstruction era, when our ancestors became taxpayers and individuals on census records instead of property.

Taylor's fifth-grade class took a trip to Ellis Island to help them understand the great wave of immigration that took place between the Civil War and the First World War. I was surprised at how many of the families in her class had some ancestor who came through Ellis Island. It was so common that my daughter began to feel left out and started pressing me for relatives that had come through the Island. As we walked around the great hall with displays of baggage and points of departure and numbers of immigrants per year, I found another display on immigration. It was a display on an earlier wave—the forced migration we know as the slave trade. I pointed to 1740 and told Taylor that 1740 is the year when, we believe, our first known ancestor came to America. "Your grandparents' grandparents were all in America by the end of the Civil War—before Ellis Island opened," I told her. We are another American story.

Ellis Island is Taylor's story, too. It is the story of some of her friends and classmates. It is the story of this country and our legacy of open doors, a legacy that is sorely tested today. Ellis Island was a tremendous enterprise, yet for all the processing and examining, only 1 percent of the hopeful immigrants were refused entry. Imagine if just one member of a family was denied entry because of illness. Most likely the oldest daughter would also be sent back home to accompany that sick family member. As the oldest daughter of my own family, I could easily identify with the dashed hopes of a girl in that situation. She would return to the old country to live out her life as a poor relation to people struggling to farm depleted land.

Sadly, the ability to walk through the doors of Ellis Island—imagining what it would be like to put everything you own in sewn-together quilts and ride in steerage to find a new life—was, for a while, almost lost. Thankfully, some of the deteriorating buildings at Ellis Island have been restored along with access to the main hall. It took millions of privately raised dollars and a campaign led by former Chrysler CEO Lee Iacocca to do it, but Ellis Island was saved.

A generation ago, the history of destitute immigrants was not considered worth preserving. Traditional history focuses on the wealthy and the powerful, the wars of kings and presidents. It is refreshing and revealing that history now looks at the fate of poor immigrants, women in pioneer towns, Native Americans whose way of life was destroyed by the Westward Expansion. One of the remarkable examples of today's new focus in history is a current exhibit at the Smithsonian Museum called "America: After the Revolution," which includes examples of the homelife and culture of Americans of different races, classes, and walks of life. The exhibit features homes built and occupied by Native Americans, by African slaves, by a poor, white farmer, and by a wealthy merchant. It shows the implements used for homemaking, the great variety of utensils used for cooking and eating, and sleeping arrangements from woven pallets to cornhusk mattresses to feather beds. It is a simple exhibit, yet so powerful in its acknowledgment of the complex tapestry that was and is America.

When we know our history, we can place ourselves in context in a long stream of triumph and suffering, an ebb and flow of human events and achievements. No child or adult should look at the history of this nation and have to ask, "What does this have to do with me?" No one should have to wonder whether his or her people have a history, a legacy to claim and celebrate.

I am richer for learning about the hopes and dreams of those who came to this country by way of Ellis Island, and the children of those who came through Ellis Island are richer for knowing the struggle to overcome slavery and its aftereffects. My mother was committed to telling that story, and we need to continue to tell all the stories of every stream, every patch in the quilt that is the United States of America. When we understand our history as an American people—intertwined, intermingled, and blessed with powerful stories of triumph over adversity and deep commitment to ideals—our belief in what is possible for this nation can only increase.

Work Is Love
Made Visible

Whether she was employed in a paying job, making a home for her extended family, or engaged in one of her many areas of volunteer service, my mother was dedicated to her work. She could always be counted on to give her best effort. She was very proud of her teaching career, and she developed a reputation as a progressive and caring educator in the Atlanta public schools. Atlanta Metropolitan College President Edwin Thompson tapped her to be one of the school's original staff members and his right hand in establishing the newly chartered institution. She brought both professional competence and a spirit of genuine commitment to meeting the needs of the AMC students.

Always innovative in her approach to solving problems, many of her most lasting contributions came in the later decades of her career, when she was no longer constrained by the bureaucracy and structures of formal employment. It was when she was able to give full range to her creativity through volunteer work that she founded Atlanta's annual Dream Jamboree, as well as the the Atlanta-Fulton County Commission on Children and Youth and its Listening to Youth program. She said of that period in her life that she had a working woman's schedule, but not a paying job.

Mother was constantly open to opportunities to help the causes she loved. The First Congregational Church of Atlanta was an old historic building that had, during the early part of this century, housed a number of innovative ministries in its lower level of Sunday school rooms and offices. When it was first built, it was a model facility. But the second-floor sanctuary had long since become a problem for the congregation. During the church's capital campaign to add an elevator tower, Mother happened to find herself seated next to one B. J. Hank at a dinner at the University of Notre Dame. When Mother discovered that Mr. Hank was the president of the Montgomery elevator company, she charmingly asked him to contribute an elevator to her church, one large enough to hold a casket. Remarkably, he agreed, and the elevator tower was completed.

Although she did not live to see the centennial Olympic Games, Mother also played a tremendous role in bringing them to Atlanta. When the Olympics came to the city in 1996, it was the fulfillment of a promise to make Atlanta an international city, written in 1981 in my father's first letter announcing his intention to run for Mayor. My mother's contribution to the Games began in the early eighties when she agreed to house a young Tanzanian Olympic runner named Alphonse Swai. What began as a commitment of a few days resulted in Mother's enrolling Alphonse in junior college and providing him with a home for nearly three years. It was simply her way, but ultimately it would give Atlanta special credibility in its Olympic quest.

The bid process to become the American city began with no funding from either the city of Atlanta or the state of Georgia, but with a strategy of selling southern hospitality one Olympic delegate at a time. From all over the world, delegates were brought to my parents' home in Atlanta and served meals my parents had prepared themselves. My father would cook a large pot of his native New Orleans gumbo while Mother made a large salad and rice and supervised all of the necessary preparations to make a house ready for company— the cleaning, the table settings, arrangements of fresh flowers. She made all the delegates and their spouses feel welcome and comfortable so far away from their own homes.

Atlanta was selected as the American city of choice to host the Olympics, but nevertheless, it was assumed that the nostalgic favorite, Athens, would carry the day. So Mother joined my father in visiting International Olympic committee delegates in their own countries. Together they made special trips to see the African delegates, many of whom my father knew through the United Nations and who were aware of my parents' assistance to Alphonse and other African Olympic athletes prior to the Los Angeles games of 1984. They visited modern capitals with luxurious hotels, and rural villages without running water. In Cameroon they attended the ceremony of René Essomba's installation as chief elder of his village, and Mother was asked to dance with the women in celebration. "Her camaraderie and friendship were relayed to everyone she met, no matter their position or culture," noted Ginger Watkins, an early volunteer with the Olympics. "She related to others in a very personal and warm way." Mother attended the Olympic Games in Seoul, Barcelona, and Albertville. She sat through every formal dinner and worked the room at every cocktail reception, tirelessly promoting the virtues of Atlanta to IOC members. Her warmth and persistence ultimately helped convince the International Olympic Committee to bring the Olympic Games to Atlanta.

My mother was committed to making the Olympic Games in Atlanta accessible to people from all walks of life and all races. She was appalled by the cost of hotels and food in Barcelona, for example, which increased dramatically during the Olympics. Her outrage over this practice prompted an agreement with the Atlanta hotels not to increase prices in

1996. During the Games, I sat in the top tier at the women's gymnastics competition with a family who had driven from South Dakota to Atlanta. They were staying in a moderately priced hotel thirty miles from the Olympic core. This family was ecstatic because they could afford to attend the Olympics.

My mother was one part of the visionary team that brought the Olympics to Atlanta. Each dinner prepared, each reception attended, each delegate convinced of Atlanta's merits, was to her a labor of love for Atlanta and toward a greater humanity. She believed that Atlanta, with its history of racial cooperation and nonviolent change, had something to offer the world. The results of her work will be visible in Atlanta for generations to come.

One of the great challenges in life is finding work that is an expression of our personal love, and my mother's example has made me very sensitive to the meaning and impact of my work. When I finished law school, I couldn't imagine working for a traditional law firm, although it would have been the prudent thing to do. I didn't see the value that would come from that kind of law practice.

As a result, my career has been atypical for an attorney. I wanted to use the law to make positive change for people, which has led to some interesting jobs. I served the United Church of Christ as the director of the African mission program, although I was probably too young for the job. I attended countless meetings where I was the only person without silver hair. My job was to allocate a fixed amount of money in a time of growing need and opportunity. Despite the limited resources available to me, I was able to support innovative programs for women, encourage the United Congregational Church of Southern Africa in its opposition to apartheid, and share with the American churches the gifts and glories of our sister churches in Africa. I cherished the time I spent walking to a church service in South Africa because the road was so poor that only the occasional four-wheel-drive truck could get through. I visited villages in Uganda where the YWCA was teaching the preparation of traditional foods in new ways to improve nutrition for young children. I visited schoolchildren in Zambia who would return to school every evening for a chance to study math.

I left the Africa mission program to attend to the work of being a mother to my daughter, and thankfully, when I returned to paid work, it was work that I cared about. As the Foreign Policy advocate for the United Church of Christ it was a privilege to continue my involvement opposing apartheid in South Africa and supporting the war in Central America. As Chief of Staff to Congresswoman Cynthia McKinney, my greatest satisfaction came from work on the Earned Income Tax Credit for poor workers. The EITC is a strategy to make work pay for those on the lowest rung of the economic ladder, since the minimum wage does not provide sufficient income for even a small family to live above the poverty level.

At Planned Parenthood of Metropolitan Washington, I worked to expand access to and awareness of family-planning services for those in need. I believe that my work in these areas has helped improve the lives of others.

It is both a remonstration and a challenge to live as if your work were love made visible. Martin Luther King preached that if one was a street sweeper, one should sweep as Michelangelo painted. It was a command to find the dignity and the expression of love for humanity in the most humble labor. Dr. King was speaking to people whose choices were constricted by segregation and limited access to education. For those who are free of such restrictions and who have been provided with many choices for productive activity, it is incumbent upon us to apply our skills and talents to work that improves life for those in our midst. By teaching in schools, managing businesses, creating art and music, and designing buildings and homes, we can contribute immeasurably to the quality of our communities.

It would transform our society if everyone approached his or her work as if it were an expression of love. There would be no surly shopkeepers and indifferent salespersons. The people behind the counter at the Department of Motor Vehicles would be polite, and supervisors would hire sufficient staff and structure the process so that no one had to wait in line for three hours to get a driver's license. Banks wouldn't send credit cards to people who are already heavily in debt.

Gun manufacturers would place safety locks on hunting rifles and no one would make cheap "Saturday-night specials" or sell semiautomatic weapons to civilians. The tobacco companies would have shifted into alternative products as soon as their research revealed the health consequences of smoking, and no one would have advertised smoking to children.

At this stage in my life, most of my contributions to society have been through my paid work, although I am involved as a volunteer as well. As I struggle to raise a child, hold down a job, and remain involved in my community, I am awed by the range of activities my mother participated in while raising four children.

Our society is in the process of making virtually every healthy person work at a paying job. At the same time, we are exhorting Americans to volunteer. But in order to do so, people need discretionary time, time that is now going into paying work. We are losing the quality of life that is generated by neighbors who attend community meetings, who serve on the PTA, who lead Scout troops, who teach Sunday School, and who organize grand civic endeavors like my mother's Dream Jamboree.

One of the many challenges for American society, as the world's model market-based culture, is to find a way to value and reward these intangible contributions. Our vital civic culture was once able to exist because inefficiency was tolerated. We are now steadily wringing the inefficiency out of our companies, our shops, and our government. As employees are driven to better and better efficiency, the society outside of work pays the cost. My city, for example, has a new administration that is bent on improving service and efficiency. That is a good thing. But it also means that our Girl Scout troop lost a leader for forty girls. The pressures of her job working for the city eliminated the inefficiency that had previously allowed her to make a few calls or type a notice for the troop on her lunch break. She no longer has a lunch break.

The Bible says, "where your treasure is, there your heart will be also." The allocation of money does reflect a statement of values, of what work we value in this nation. There are platitudes about the value of motherhood, but women who raise children and work outside the home are often penalized twice, once with lower earnings at the job, and again by the Internal Revenue Service. The salaries of some basketball players could employ the average teacher for hundreds of years. There is always a call for churches to do more to help the indigent—but who are the church workers? In my church, it's the healthy retirees. Working parents sustain many of the children's programs, but outreach work is generally done by older members whose children have grown up and left home.

As we raise the retirement age in this country, we also reduce the volunteer workforce in our churches, museums, and other labor-intensive charities. Connie Stevens, the volunteer who heads the food and clothing ministry at our church, helps forty families each week obtain groceries and serviceable clothes. This ministry recycles household furnishings to families who have suffered losses from fire, for example, or to formerly homeless families who have finally been assigned a subsidized apartment. One woman who comes by the church food pantry every month had been living on Social Security and raising her grandson who was born as the result of a rape that left her daughter infected with the AIDS virus. I drove this woman to her home with groceries and a bag of clean clothes for her grandson, and I thought, "How does she survive?" Connie Stevens may make the difference as to whether she survives.

What if Social Security were to recognize volunteer hours? For that matter, what if stay-at-home mothers or fathers received Social Security credit for the years they stayed out of the paid workforce to concentrate on parenting? What if people below a certain income received tax credits for taking on a volunteer responsibility with a not-for-profit organization like a homeless shelter or literacy program? In a society where money is everything, people who serve for the good of others and for the good of their communities pay a very real price in economic insecurity. If someone like Connie Stevens becomes ill, her medical bills will not be discounted because of her years of dedicated volunteerism.

It is said that in our society, we know the cost of everything and the value of nothing. We pay an enormous price when the compassion and understanding of love are absent from our work and civic life, losing a sense that dedication, loyalty and sacrifice for the good of others will be rewarded or even acknowledged.

We need community efforts that occur without reference to profit motive and market value. We need people working within the public, private, and nonprofit sectors who guide their decisions in a framework that includes the expression of their best selves. If everyone would use his or her life energy to express a love for humanity, this would be a better world.

It takes courage to live that way, to resist the cynicism that we encounter every day. The path of least resistance is to go along with the crowd, to collect the paycheck at the end of the week and avoid anything controversial, anything that might expose us to harsh public criticism. We are vulnerable when we care about the impact of what we are doing, when we work hard to create something—a new college, a citywide career fair, or a dream to bring the Olympic Games to a city best known as the home of Scarlett O'Hara.

My mother possessed that kind of courage. Her work and life were expressions of her love for her family and her community. Those who honor her and those who will never know her name all have a better life because her work was love made visible.

DIE WITH GRACE
AND COURAGE

For my first thirty-five years of life, my mother showed me how to live guided by sound moral values. Much too soon, she was to show me how to die in the same way. In 1991, after a baby shower for my sister Lisa, my mother was taken to the emergency room complaining of severe intestinal pain. The doctors at Crawford Long Hospital identified a tumor in her colon that was diagnosed as malignant. An operation was performed almost immediately.

Mother was only fifty-nine years old, the youngest member of her family. Her own mother was still healthy and active. And Mother looked and acted like the picture of health: On a family vacation to the Bahamas the previous summer, she had beaten her son-in-law at tennis. I was stunned by her illness. I had always taken for granted that my mother would be around well into her nineties.

With characteristic determination, Mother fought the disease, which was discovered at an advanced stage. She endured two operations and several rounds of chemotherapy. When her beautiful hair came out from the treatments, she bought colorful berets and decorated them with pins and sequins. Her strength of will sustained all her children and the members of her extended family, and it gave us hope, even confidence, that she would overcome this threat to her life.

Throughout her battle with cancer, Mother continued to care for and nurture her family. She delayed her second surgery to be present for the November birth of Lisa's second child, Lena. She would not allow her life to be run by fear of dying: her priority was to see her new grandchild and to provide support for her daughter. Mother gained strength from the joy and satisfaction of fulfilling her roles as mother and grandmother. After the surgery, Mother and Lisa spent the spring hanging out together with the baby, visiting shops, strolling in parks, watching the dogwood trees bloom, and savoring the miracles of life.

When the Atlanta chapter of the United Negro College Fund asked to honor Mother with a scholarship in her name, initially, Mother was hurt. Given her competitive nature, she had every intention of defeating the cancer, and she believed that scholarships were usually named for people who had died. She, on the other hand, was very much alive!

But she knew that Billye Aaron, the regional director for UNCF, had only good intentions, and she decided that if she was to be honored in this way, she would attend the formal dinner held for her dressed as a Queen. She purchased a special outfit, a shimmering gold African-inspired dress with a tall crownlike headdress to mask the loss of her thick, rich hair. It was a bittersweet occasion, a little like attending one's own funeral, but if she found the occasion disconcerting, she gave no sign of it. She was charming to all her well-wishers, and even vivacious throughout the dinner. Her acceptance of the honor of the Jean Childs Young Scholarship Fund was made with tremendous grace.

After nearly six months of treatment, Mother was declared cancer-free. She began to regain her old energy level, so much so that the Atlanta Friendship Force approached her about leading their first delegation to South Africa. The Friendship Force was a nonprofit group devoted to building bridges of understanding between Americans and the citizens of other nations. Mother had participated in the first visit of Atlantans to what was then Soviet Georgia. Despite her very recent illness and the risk of overtaxing her energy, Mother was eager to help promote intercultural, international, and interracial understanding between America and South Africa.

Each of the participants in the delegation was responsible for his or her own travel expenses, a sum that could have paid for a comparable number of days in a luxurious spa or resort. After Mother's ordeal, one might expect that she would prefer a week of self indulgence to such a rigorous trip, but her spirit and sense of purpose was always enriched by this kind of encounter.

Mother and an interracial delegation of Atlantans went to the major cities of South Africa, to a game park, and to a traditional Ndebele village with its colorfully painted homes. The focus of the trip, however, was Cape Town, the country's legislative capital and Atlanta's designated sister city. Mother and her friend Earlene Harris, who had been charged with looking after her on the trip, often found themselves serving as cultural interpreters. When one of the Atlantans made an insensitive comment about the poverty of black South Africans and why they were less industrious than the whites, Mother treated the group to a lecture on the history of South African apartheid and the impact of systematically stripping land and wealth from the country's black population. She also persuaded the group to commit to raise $10,000 to enable a multiracial South African group to visit Atlanta.

In Cape Town, the Atlanta delegation was invited by the AME church and Reverend McKinley Young, who had served one of the larger churches in Atlanta and was serving as the AME Bishop of South Africa, to join in a songfest. There,

Mother met Reverend Andrew Lewin and his wife, Angeline. They were a strikingly handsome couple with a large brood of bright, attractive children. Mother commented that her own husband was a minister named Andrew. She discovered another similarity: Angeline had been diagnosed with cancer of the colon. But in South Africa, there was no treatment available to her, and she had been sent home to allow the disease to run its course. Immediately, Mother insisted that Angeline come to Atlanta with her where Mother would arrange and pay for Angeline to receive treatment from her own doctors. Mother saw that she could easily have been in the same position as Angeline. The coincidence was too great; she felt called to help.

Rather than use her illness as a legitimate reason to do less for others, Mother seemed to be compelled to do more. She remained true to her beliefs, even under tremendous stress of such a serious illness. Even severely tested, her character proved true and pure.

Angeline lived in my parents' home for several months, and was treated by Mother's physicians. Mother paid all the bills, and recruited members of her own support network as support for Angeline. Angeline was dignified and always gracious. Mother's friend Sammy Bacote was once overcharged by a parking attendant while taking Angeline to see the doctor. Angeline pointed this out immediately, and insisted that Sammy go back to have the matter corrected. For her family's sake, Angeline accepted the kindness and charity of strangers, but she could not tolerate the spending of one dollar more on her than was absolutely necessary.

When Mother had arranged all that medical science could do for Angeline, Andrew Lewin came to Atlanta and took his wife home to spend her last months with her children.

In 1993, my entire family gathered at my parents' home for Christmas. Unbeknownst to us, Mother had begun to feel ill again. She sat quietly, reflectively, taking in the scene as her children and grandchildren and friends filled the house, sharing gifts and admiring her ten-foot Christmas tree with its crystal decorations. She bought special red and black outfits for her three grandchildren and made an appointment with a photographer to have a formal family portrait taken. In the photograph, she is standing over Taylor, Kemet, and Lena like a guardian angel. Somehow, the children seemed to have sensed the importance of the picture. Each one looks sweet and serene. It is a photograph I will always treasure, and the kind of little gift Mother continued to give in the months to come, finding small ways to help us prepare to deal with her death.

Only Mother's oldest, closest friends knew how difficult it was for her to leave this life and move to the next. Sitting with her friend Sammy Bacote in her special, yellow upholstered rocking chair, she complained gently, "Cancer is a terrible thing. I don't see why God made cancer." Sammy told her that some good had come as a result of her illness: it had brought her family even closer together. Her relationship with her son Bo was closer than it had been since he was a small boy, and people around the city were praying for her. Every evening at six o'clock, a prayer group met on her behalf, and some people had even come back to their faith because of her illness. Mother reflected for a moment and asked sadly, "Couldn't God have found another way?"

In my presence, she was always brave and determined, though I did see her grow weary. In her last months she would tolerate pain, forgoing medication, so that her head could be clear for visitors, especially her grandchildren. She wanted to savor every moment with her family and she wanted us to see her as she really was, rather than vague and heavily medicated. She never showed any doubt or any loss of faith. Her concern was for others—for her husband, her children, her family, and her projects.

My parent's fortieth anniversary came while Mother had been in the hospital for more than two months. This milestone was a testament to the faithful way she had lived her life, and we wanted to observe it in a special way. The entire family gathered at the hospital: Mother's four children, three grandchildren, her brothers and sister, her mother, nieces, nephews, and family friends. In the visitors' lounge, a caterer set up a lovely buffet dinner and cake. The lounge and Mother's own room were always filled with flowers sent by well-wishers from around the country.

Once everyone had gathered, my father brought Mother

to the lounge in a wheelchair. She was dressed in a lovely blue caftan. We sat quietly, eagerly, expectantly, while my father talked about their four decades of marriage, and what it had meant to him and to all of us to have Mother's love, care, and support. When it was Mother's time to speak, she smiled weakly and whispered, "I love you all, thank you." Taylor and Kemet had moved to be near her and she stroked their heads. Then, with Mother obviously exhausted from the effort, my father rolled her back to her room and bed.

Later that evening, Mother's spiritual pastor, the Reverend Paul Smith, sat with the members of the immediate family. Paul has made ministering to the dying and to their loved ones a particular focus of his work. He prayed with us and asked us whether we thought our Mother was dying. He told us that Mother's will remained so strong that while she had made her peace with death, she wanted her loved ones as well to be ready to face the end.

On September 16, 1994, my mother passed on to glory, to what Christians believe is a better place and a better life that never ends. My sister Lisa and I handled the arrangements with the funeral home and selected a casket and a blue silk dress for Mother's body. We held a private family viewing and I was not at all eager to participate. But when I looked into the casket, I could see that the spirit of my mother was no longer there; it had not died but had gone where spirits of the faithful go, affirming my belief in angels.

Mother's "Standing Committee of the House" had to organize one, last event, a celebration of the life of Jean Childs Young. Her beloved church was too small to accommodate all those who wanted to attend the service, so we held it at the site of the Dream Jamboree, the auditorium of the Atlanta Civic Center. My husband arranged the casket in the center of the stage, surrounded by flowers like an altar. A choir of students from three Atlanta high schools sang hymns of joy and faith. My father was determined that the service would be about my mother's life, rather than about her life with him. Consequently, the celebrants were all women who had worked and served with Mother on her many projects.

No single person knew or could tell all the facets of my mother's life, and everyone present learned something new that day about her extraordinary years of committed service to her family, her community, and the international community. The congregation of more than two thousand included people from every neighborhood in Atlanta and from all over the nation. International diplomats and friends and neighbors laughed and cried together in celebration of a great spirit and servant of God.

I will never understand why my mother died so young. But despite leaving us too soon, she left behind a treasury of love and service that many could not have achieved in several lifetimes. Her legacy lives on in her children and grandchildren, and, if you have been touched by any of these lessons—in you.

ACKNOWLEDGMENTS

The portrait of my mother and her values was accomplished with the assistance of many wonderful and generous people. My mother, Jean Young, wrote for us a personal book, *Reflections*, which kept this project grounded in her voice. My father, Andrew Young, shared many stories without pushing his own interpretation of them. My siblings, Paula Shelton, Lisa Alston, and Bo Young, as well as my aunts Cora Moore and Norma DePaur were generous with their memories, as were my mother's dear friend and sister-in-law, Sonjia Young, and Sammy Bacote. Carolyn Young, Marion Jones, Sue Ross, Alice

Johnson, Dan Moore, Earline Harris, and Paul and Carol Muldawer also shared their stories.

My dear husband, Tony Stanley, read the manuscript as it evolved and gave his unwavering moral support to this project.

I would also like to thank the Auburn Avenue Research Library on African-American History and Culture for generous access to the Andrew Young papers, and Sue Ross for her assistance in assembling appropriate photographs.

This book would not have been written without the faith and encouragement of my agent, Lawrence Jordan.

My editor, Wendy Hubbert, kept the text true to the vision.

I am grateful for all the goodwill people all over the world have shown our family over the years, and for the many people who encouraged me to write this book.

ABOUT THE PHOTOGRAPHS

Page ii. Jean Young and daughter Andrea, 1956. (Young Family Collection)

Page vi. Jean Childs in high school. (Idella Childs Collection)

Page xiv. Jean, Andrew, Andrea, and Lisa. New York 1957. (Young Family Collection)

Page 8. Jean Childs and Andrew Young at May Queen Dinner, Manchester College, 1953. (Young Family Collection)

Page 24. Jean and Andrew at their wedding reception in his parents' home in New Orleans, 1954. (Young Family Collection)

Page 40. Honoring Nelson Mandela in Atlanta: Andrew Young, Xernona Clayton, Nelson Mandela, Jean Young, Angeline Lewin, Lisa Young Alston, Bo Young. (Susan J. Ross)

Page 54. Love Ladies Tennis Team: Jo Robeson, Jean Young, Sonjia Young. (Young Family Collection)

Page 70. Andrew, Andrea, and Jean Young at the Central Congregational Church, New Orleans, 1955. (Young Family Collection)

Page 84. Jean Young at the first Atlanta mayoral campaign. (Jonathan Tice)

Page 98. Bo Young, Rosalynn Carter, Jean Young at an International Year of the Child event, 1979. (Rick Reinhard)

Page 114. Jean Young with children in Zimbabwe. (Young Family Collection)

Page 130. Jean Young gives direction to Dream Jamboree volunteers. (Susan J. Ross)

Page 148. Jean, Andrea, and Lisa Young, 1962. (Young Family Collection)

Page 160. Tony Stanley, Andrea Young, Taylor Stanley, Lisa, Kemet, and Douglas Alston, Idella Childs, Jean, Andrew, and Bo Young, Paula and Hilary Shelton in Mother's new living room, 1990. (Thomas Dorsey)

Page 172. Jean, Taylor, Andrea, 1988. (Susan J. Ross)

Page 182. The Childs family: Norma, Norman Sr., Jean, Idella, Norman Jr., Bill, Cora, circa 1940. (Idella Childs Collection)

Page 192. Jean Young receiving honorary doctorate from Manchester College. (Young Family Collection)

Page 204. Andrew Young, Jean, and Norma Childs. Germany, 1953. (Idella Childs Collection)

Page 216. Dr. Benjamin Mays and Jean Young speak to public school students. (Young Family Collection)

Page 228. Jean and Andrew Young at a parade celebrating Atlanta's selection as host city for the Olympic Games, 1990. (Susan J. Ross) Page 240. Jean's photo with her grandchildren: Jean and Andrew Young, Idella Childs, Lena and Kemet Alston, Taylor Stanley, Christmas 1993. (Thomas Dorsey) Page 250. Jean and Andrew Young attend a reception in Washington, D.C. (Young Family Collection)

ANDREA YOUNG is an attorney, public policy analyst, activist, and writer who collaborated with her father on his memoir *An Easy Burden* (HarperCollins, 1996). A former legislative aide and speechwriter for Senator Edward Kennedy, vice-president of Planned Parenthood of Metropolitan Washington, D.C., and program director for the United Church of Christ, she has conducted global education and advocacy workshops and served as the keynote speaker for educational, civic, and religious institutions. She lives with her husband, the Reverend A. Knighton Stanley, and their daughter in Washington, D.C.